# Advance Praise

## From the Inside Out

The Reverend Dr. Andriette Earl is gifting the world a true gem. Her messages "from the inside out" demonstrate her own commitment to activating the One's power of the inner life to direct and enhance external actions, both individually and within community. She invites us to join in on her journey, in our own way, of being and living profound metaphysical principles and practices with integrity. I am confident you will enjoy this pilgrimage toward multidimensional wholeness, as I have.

— **The Reverend Will Coleman, Ph.D.**
Associate Professor of Theology and World Religions,
Interdenominational Theological Center;
Adjunct Professor, Holmes Institute;
Adjunct Professor, Johnnie Coleman Theological Seminary

*From the Inside Out* is a warm healing voice to a cold wounded world. Rev. Dr. Andriette Earl draws on her spiritual and sacred mission to call each of us into our own magnificence and golden glory without apology. Centered in her own musings, reflections, and spiritual insights, this book will lead you to the higher vibration we all need and deserve.

—**Dr. Shawn Ginwright**
Jerome T. Murphy Professor of Practice,
Harvard Graduate School of Education;
Chief Executive Officer, Flourish Agenda, Inc.

Rev. Dr. Andrette Earl's transformative new book, *From the Inside Out*, is a profound exploration of the human experience through the lens of love. With wisdom that radiates from the pages, she delves into the essence of human emotion, unraveling its layers and demonstrating how love can be a guiding force in our lives, fostering connection and understanding. She skillfully weaves narratives that inspire and uplift readers with the practical application of the principles of spirituality. *From the Inside Out* is a masterpiece that will leave an indelible mark on the hearts and minds of all who embark on its transformative journey.

— **Soni Cantrell-Smith**
Spiritual Leader, Centers for Spiritual Living

Rev. Dr. Andriette Earl has consistently been a voice of inspiration, divine reason, and prophetic zeal, and this shows up in her writings. As you read her words, you may move seamlessly from feeling a comforting embrace to hearing a visionary call to sensing a deep contemplation that causes you to sit with a sentence for some time before moving on to the next. This is evidence of a master of the craft. Rev. Andriette stewards the power of her word with the kind of ineffable precision only afforded to a mystic of the 21st century. Prepare to have your life changed by reading what she has gifted you.

— **Rev. Dr. Raymont Anderson**
Founding Minister and Spiritual Director,
The Center for Spiritually Integrated Arts

Rev. Dr. Andriette Earl takes us on a rich inward journey of awakening. These exquisite offerings are keys to living a life of deep meaning and infinite happiness. Enjoy the ride!

— **Dr. John B. Waterhouse**
Former President and Field Leader,
Centers for Spiritual Living

Rev. Dr. Andriette Earl makes it clear: The most important changes happen internally and require our full commitment to understanding and applying spiritual principles. No matter where you are on your growth journey, there are priceless gems in these pages that you can use to get in touch with your spiritual truth. The good news is that her writing makes it feel completely possible to take on this challenge—and win.

—**Dr. Tracy Brown, RScP**
author of *I Turn to Prayer*

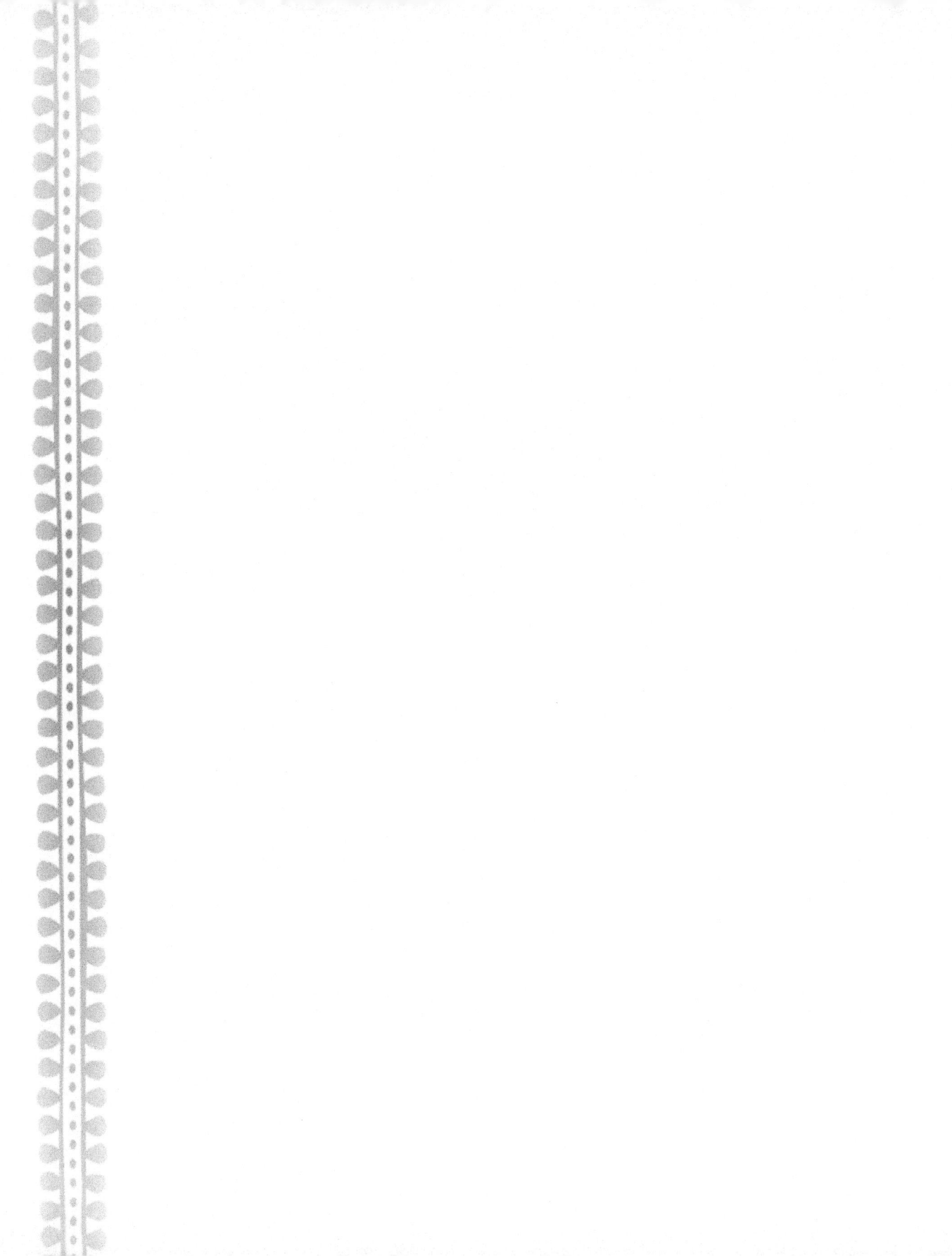

# From the Inside Out

## A Continuing Spiritual Evolution

Rev. Dr. Andriette Earl

Foreword by Susan L. Taylor

Copyright 2024, Andriette Earl

All rights reserved.

No part of this book may be reproduced in any form
without permission in writing from the publisher, except for
brief quotations embodied in critical articles or reviews.

Spiritual Living Press is an imprint of Centers for Spiritual Living
Lakewood, Colorado 80226
www.Shop.CSL.org

Printed in the United States of America
Published 2024

Editor: Julie Mierau, JM Wordsmith
Cover Design: Holli Sharp, Centers for Spiritual Living
Interior Design/Typesetting: Stephanie Finne, Centers for Spiritual Living

ISBN paperback: 978-1-956198-44-7

ISBN eBook: 978-1-956198-45-4

# Dedication

With great respect for my ancestors on whose shoulders I stand, I am honored to represent and embody our legacy of faith, awareness, and love for our people.

In loving memory of my familial trinity: my Granny, Ada Gus; my mother, Nan; and my godmother, Katie. Thank you for pouring into me. I pray I represent you well.

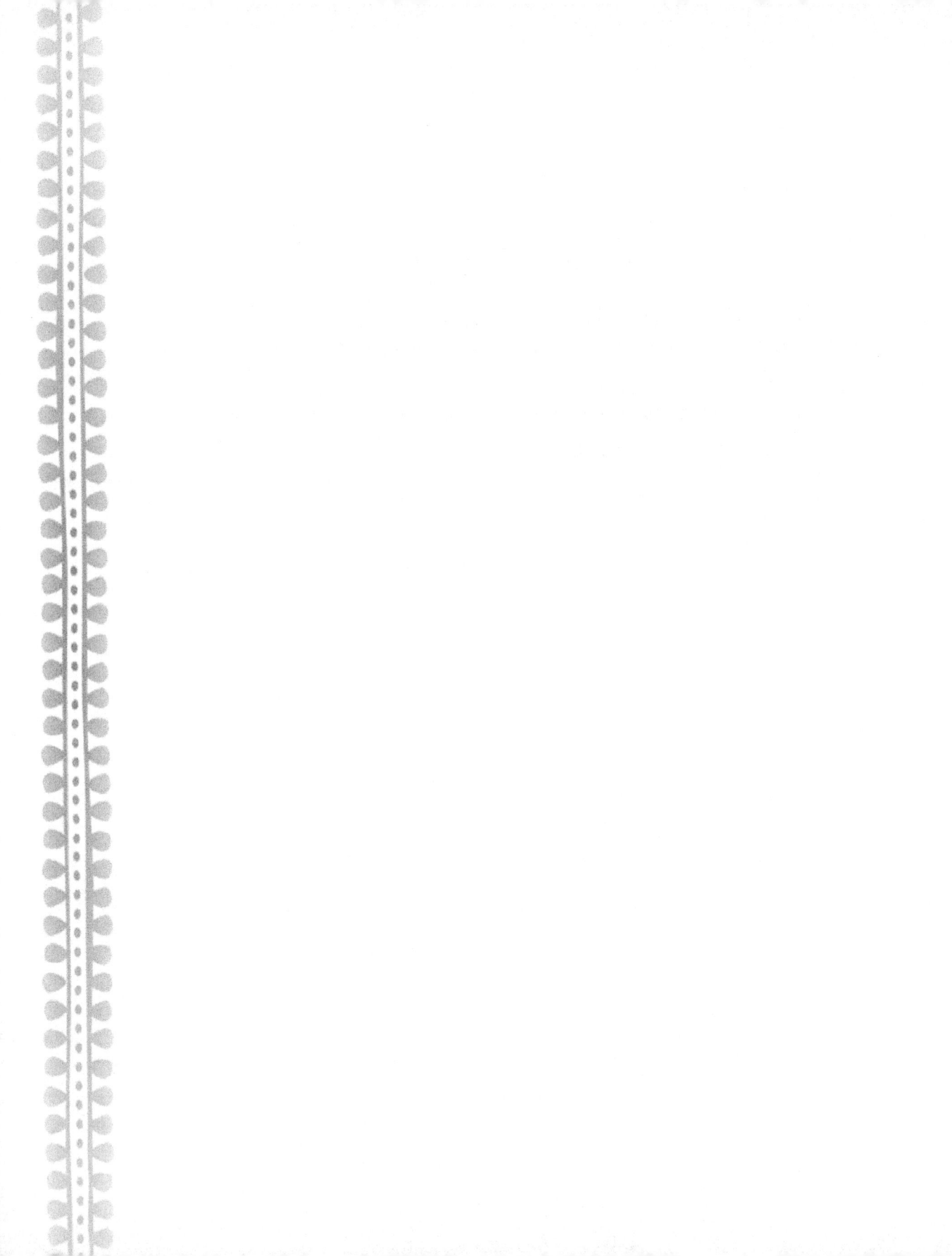

# Acknowledgments

I am thankful for all the love, support, and assistance I had in compiling this book. There were so many angels over this past decade—too many to name or number—who blessed me and this project in the most perfect ways.

I am especially grateful to Rev. Jack Elliott for his encouragement, faith in me, and steadfast support over the past forty-two years. From my very first sermon, in his pulpit (circa 1986), through the co-founding of Heart and Soul in 2009, to my commitment to write this book, he has been there for me, always coaxing me to lead and share from my heart.

This book would not have been possible without publisher Holli Sharp, a brilliant, creative, and compassionate professional. I am grateful for her trust, patience, and compassionate leadership.

I cannot find words to fully express my gratitude to Julie Mierau for her clarity, expert editing, and tutelage. She honored my voice, and I am so grateful for her guidance. I am honored to have the benefit of her wisdom, skill, and friendship.

I am deeply indebted to my beloved sister, Valda Earl-Southall—the best sister ever—for her love and understanding. Her presence blesses my life. Her assistance with many of my personal responsibilities freed me to stay focused on writing.

My deepest appreciation is for my Heart and Soul Center of Light community—my heart home. Because of them, I am who I am today and do what I do. Because of them, I began writing for *Science of Mind* magazine. They are a constant source of love and joy. They beckon me to my greatest yet to be. Heart and Soul is the wind beneath my wings.

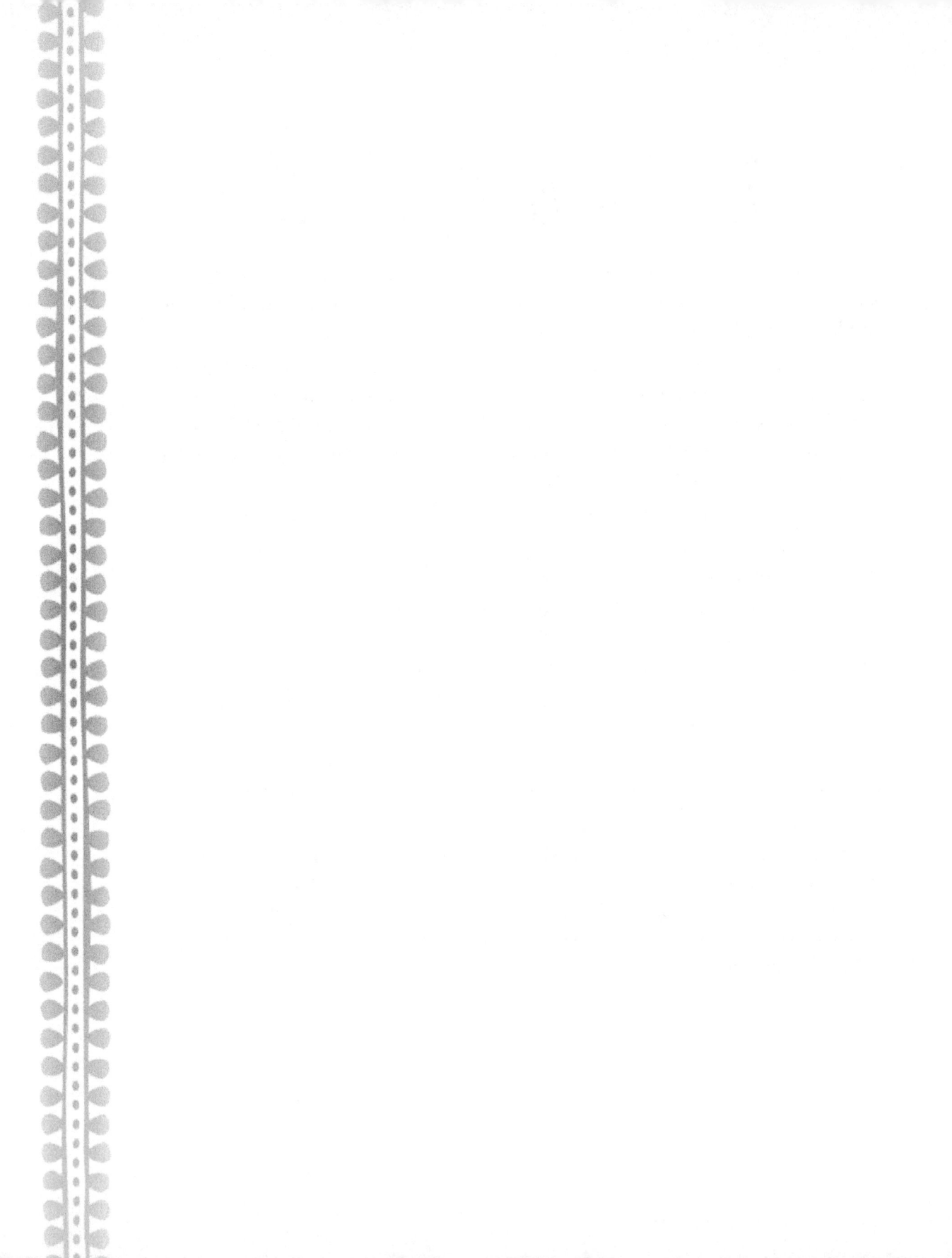

# Table of Contents

Dedication . . . . . . . . . . . . . . . . . . . . . . . . . . . . . . . . . . . . i
Acknowledgments . . . . . . . . . . . . . . . . . . . . . . . . . . . . . . . iii
Editor's Note . . . . . . . . . . . . . . . . . . . . . . . . . . . . . . . . . . xiii
Foreword . . . . . . . . . . . . . . . . . . . . . . . . . . . . . . . . . . . . . xv
Introduction. . . . . . . . . . . . . . . . . . . . . . . . . . . . . . . . . . . xvii

**Section 1—Love: From the Inside Out. . . . . . . . . . . . . .1**
Deeper in Love. . . . . . . . . . . . . . . . . . . . . . . . . . . . . . . . . 2
Partners . . . . . . . . . . . . . . . . . . . . . . . . . . . . . . . . . . . . . 3
Human *and* Divine . . . . . . . . . . . . . . . . . . . . . . . . . . . . 4
You Had It All the Time . . . . . . . . . . . . . . . . . . . . . . . . 5
The Heart of the Matter . . . . . . . . . . . . . . . . . . . . . . . . 6
Celebrating *Our* History. . . . . . . . . . . . . . . . . . . . . . . . 7
Daily Resurrection . . . . . . . . . . . . . . . . . . . . . . . . . . . . 8
It Will Be Ours. . . . . . . . . . . . . . . . . . . . . . . . . . . . . . . 9
Joy Cometh in the Morning . . . . . . . . . . . . . . . . . . . . 11
Keys to the Kingdom. . . . . . . . . . . . . . . . . . . . . . . . . . 12
Solid as a Rock. . . . . . . . . . . . . . . . . . . . . . . . . . . . . . 13
I Pray Love. . . . . . . . . . . . . . . . . . . . . . . . . . . . . . . . . 14
Love's in Need of Love . . . . . . . . . . . . . . . . . . . . . . . 16
A New Heaven . . . . . . . . . . . . . . . . . . . . . . . . . . . . . 18
Magnetize Infinite Possibility. . . . . . . . . . . . . . . . . . .20
Trusting Truth . . . . . . . . . . . . . . . . . . . . . . . . . . . . . . 21
We're in this Love Together . . . . . . . . . . . . . . . . . . . 22
Bravely Live Your Divine Truth . . . . . . . . . . . . . . . . 23
The Courage To Be Vulnerable. . . . . . . . . . . . . . . . . 24

**Section 2—Faith: From the Inside Out** . . . . . . . . . . . **25**
   What Are You Doing for Others? . . . . . . . . . . . . . . . . . . . . . . .26
   Be Whole . . . . . . . . . . . . . . . . . . . . . . . . . . . . . . . . . . . . . . . . . . .27
   Give Thanks . . . . . . . . . . . . . . . . . . . . . . . . . . . . . . . . . . . . . . . .28
   It's Already Done . . . . . . . . . . . . . . . . . . . . . . . . . . . . . . . . . . . .29
   Pay Attention to Divine Frequency . . . . . . . . . . . . . . . . . . . . . .30
   This Far by Faith . . . . . . . . . . . . . . . . . . . . . . . . . . . . . . . . . . . . .31
   The Joy of Answered Prayer . . . . . . . . . . . . . . . . . . . . . . . . . . .33
   Ancient Wisdom . . . . . . . . . . . . . . . . . . . . . . . . . . . . . . . . . . . .35
   Eye on the Prize . . . . . . . . . . . . . . . . . . . . . . . . . . . . . . . . . . . . .37
   Secure in God . . . . . . . . . . . . . . . . . . . . . . . . . . . . . . . . . . . . . . .38
   A Bubble of Our Choosing . . . . . . . . . . . . . . . . . . . . . . . . . . . .39
   Playing Full-out in Faith . . . . . . . . . . . . . . . . . . . . . . . . . . . . . .40
   *Tomorrowland* . . . . . . . . . . . . . . . . . . . . . . . . . . . . . . . . . . . . . .42
   I Didn't Falter . . . . . . . . . . . . . . . . . . . . . . . . . . . . . . . . . . . . . . .44
   Know Exactly Who You Are . . . . . . . . . . . . . . . . . . . . . . . . . . .45
   Freedom Treks . . . . . . . . . . . . . . . . . . . . . . . . . . . . . . . . . . . . . .46
   It's Up to Me . . . . . . . . . . . . . . . . . . . . . . . . . . . . . . . . . . . . . . . .48

**Section 3—Oneness: From the Inside Out** . . . . . . . . **49**
   We *Are* the Ones . . . . . . . . . . . . . . . . . . . . . . . . . . . . . . . . . . . .50
   Just Us . . . . . . . . . . . . . . . . . . . . . . . . . . . . . . . . . . . . . . . . . . . . .51
   Break through to Boldness . . . . . . . . . . . . . . . . . . . . . . . . . . . .52
   Imagine Me . . . . . . . . . . . . . . . . . . . . . . . . . . . . . . . . . . . . . . . .53
   View from Afar . . . . . . . . . . . . . . . . . . . . . . . . . . . . . . . . . . . . .55
   Willing to Forgive . . . . . . . . . . . . . . . . . . . . . . . . . . . . . . . . . . .56
   The Flow of Divine Choreography . . . . . . . . . . . . . . . . . . . . .57
   Set Everyone Free . . . . . . . . . . . . . . . . . . . . . . . . . . . . . . . . . . .58
   Centers of God's Consciousness . . . . . . . . . . . . . . . . . . . . . . .60

Namaste: God in Me Sees God in You . . . . . . . . . . . . . . . . . 61
Carefully Taught . . . . . . . . . . . . . . . . . . . . . . . . . . . . . . . . . 63
Holy Encounter . . . . . . . . . . . . . . . . . . . . . . . . . . . . . . . . . . 65
Calling All Good People . . . . . . . . . . . . . . . . . . . . . . . . . . . 66
All One . . . . . . . . . . . . . . . . . . . . . . . . . . . . . . . . . . . . . . . . . 67
The Gift of Compassion . . . . . . . . . . . . . . . . . . . . . . . . . . . 68
Better Together . . . . . . . . . . . . . . . . . . . . . . . . . . . . . . . . . . 70
The North Star . . . . . . . . . . . . . . . . . . . . . . . . . . . . . . . . . . 71
Our Roots: Rebooting Our Awareness . . . . . . . . . . . . . . . 72

## Section 4—Begin: From the Inside Out . . . . . . . . . . 73
In the Beginning . . . . . . . . . . . . . . . . . . . . . . . . . . . . . . . . . 74
Through the Fire . . . . . . . . . . . . . . . . . . . . . . . . . . . . . . . . 75
Shift into the Flow . . . . . . . . . . . . . . . . . . . . . . . . . . . . . . . 76
Together … At Last . . . . . . . . . . . . . . . . . . . . . . . . . . . . . . 77
Begin Now . . . . . . . . . . . . . . . . . . . . . . . . . . . . . . . . . . . . . 78
*Vivir Bien* . . . . . . . . . . . . . . . . . . . . . . . . . . . . . . . . . . . . . . 79
One with the Father . . . . . . . . . . . . . . . . . . . . . . . . . . . . . 80
Taking a Powerful Stand . . . . . . . . . . . . . . . . . . . . . . . . . . 81
Awakened, Arisen, and Free . . . . . . . . . . . . . . . . . . . . . . . 82
Our Bright Light . . . . . . . . . . . . . . . . . . . . . . . . . . . . . . . . 83
Kintsugi 2020 . . . . . . . . . . . . . . . . . . . . . . . . . . . . . . . . . . . 84
New Year, New Me . . . . . . . . . . . . . . . . . . . . . . . . . . . . . . 85
When I Think of Home . . . . . . . . . . . . . . . . . . . . . . . . . . . 86

## Section 5—Shift: From the Inside Out . . . . . . . . . . 87
On Point . . . . . . . . . . . . . . . . . . . . . . . . . . . . . . . . . . . . . . . 88
Now I See It . . . . . . . . . . . . . . . . . . . . . . . . . . . . . . . . . . . . 89

Ask, Seek, Knock . . . . . . . . . . . . . . . . . . . . . . . . . . . . . . . . . . . 90
A Simple Choice. . . . . . . . . . . . . . . . . . . . . . . . . . . . . . . . . . . . 91
Our Perfect T.O.O.L. . . . . . . . . . . . . . . . . . . . . . . . . . . . . . . . . 92
Ready for Love and Learning . . . . . . . . . . . . . . . . . . . . . . . . . . 93
Reframe, Repot, and Bloom . . . . . . . . . . . . . . . . . . . . . . . . . . 94
Mind Your Mind . . . . . . . . . . . . . . . . . . . . . . . . . . . . . . . . . . . 95
Heel Your Mind . . . . . . . . . . . . . . . . . . . . . . . . . . . . . . . . . . . . 96
An Inner Renovation. . . . . . . . . . . . . . . . . . . . . . . . . . . . . . . . 98
Clear Sight . . . . . . . . . . . . . . . . . . . . . . . . . . . . . . . . . . . . . . .100
Affirm It So. . . . . . . . . . . . . . . . . . . . . . . . . . . . . . . . . . . . . . .102
#MeToo: A Powerful Movement . . . . . . . . . . . . . . . . . . . . .104
Igniting Mental Conviction . . . . . . . . . . . . . . . . . . . . . . . . . .105
Speaking Truth to Doubt . . . . . . . . . . . . . . . . . . . . . . . . . . .106
Born to Be Free . . . . . . . . . . . . . . . . . . . . . . . . . . . . . . . . . . .107
A House Divided Against Itself . . . . . . . . . . . . . . . . . . . . . .108
We Believe in Freedom. . . . . . . . . . . . . . . . . . . . . . . . . . . . .109
Even in the Movies . . . . . . . . . . . . . . . . . . . . . . . . . . . . . . . . 110
Burst of Creativity. . . . . . . . . . . . . . . . . . . . . . . . . . . . . . . . . 111
Better and Better and Better . . . . . . . . . . . . . . . . . . . . . . . . 112
Mother Nature. . . . . . . . . . . . . . . . . . . . . . . . . . . . . . . . . . . . 113
Rest to Replenish . . . . . . . . . . . . . . . . . . . . . . . . . . . . . . . . . 114

## Section 6—Gratitude: From the Inside Out . . . . . . . 115
Our Gift of Ruin. . . . . . . . . . . . . . . . . . . . . . . . . . . . . . . . . . . 116
A Gift of Love and Forgiveness . . . . . . . . . . . . . . . . . . . . . . 117
My New Vision. . . . . . . . . . . . . . . . . . . . . . . . . . . . . . . . . . . . 119
When We Forgive: A New Nation . . . . . . . . . . . . . . . . . . . .120
Choose Gratitude for All Things . . . . . . . . . . . . . . . . . . . . . 121

No Complaints...........................................122

Courage to Forgive ......................................124

Accept and Bless It ......................................125

Bless It ..................................................126

Gratitude: The Cure for Amnesia.........................127

Willing to Forgive .......................................128

Miracle Divine...........................................129

Flow in Faith ............................................130

The Unified Game of Life ................................131

You Better Work It ......................................132

Divine Supply ...........................................133

**Section 7—Principle and Practice:
From the Inside Out** ................................. **135**

Look Again..............................................136

Fierce Grace Calls .......................................137

Honor the Holy .........................................138

Choose this Day to See God in All .......................139

Handle the Truth........................................140

Center Down ........................................... 141

Practice Is Key...........................................142

January Reset ...........................................143

Pure Imagination .......................................144

The Universe Awaits Your Order.........................146

Welcome! Please, Make Yourself at Home ...............147

We're Here, So Let's Do This ............................148

With Eyes Wide Open...................................150

Harriet Tubman.......................................... 151

A New Harvest..........................................152

Speak to My Heart, Lord . . . . . . . . . . . . . . . . . . . . . . . . . . . . 153

Let's Jump . . . . . . . . . . . . . . . . . . . . . . . . . . . . . . . . . . . . . . . . 155

Madiba: Imprisoned Splendor . . . . . . . . . . . . . . . . . . . . . . . 156

A Lesson in Love . . . . . . . . . . . . . . . . . . . . . . . . . . . . . . . . . . 157

Passion and Purpose Aligned . . . . . . . . . . . . . . . . . . . . . . . 158

Divine Paradox . . . . . . . . . . . . . . . . . . . . . . . . . . . . . . . . . . . 159

Wilt Thou Be Made Whole? . . . . . . . . . . . . . . . . . . . . . . . . 160

## Section 8—Vision, Voice, and Action: From the Inside Out . . . . . . . . . . . . . . . . . . . . . . . . . . 161

Step Up and Out in Faith . . . . . . . . . . . . . . . . . . . . . . . . . . 162

New Money Showing the Way . . . . . . . . . . . . . . . . . . . . . 163

A Change Gon' Come . . . . . . . . . . . . . . . . . . . . . . . . . . . . 165

Remembering the Greatest Souls . . . . . . . . . . . . . . . . . . 167

The Strategist and Tactician . . . . . . . . . . . . . . . . . . . . . . . 169

The Architect . . . . . . . . . . . . . . . . . . . . . . . . . . . . . . . . . . . . 170

The Heart of the Question . . . . . . . . . . . . . . . . . . . . . . . . . 171

Jim Crow Must Go . . . . . . . . . . . . . . . . . . . . . . . . . . . . . . . 172

Whitewashing History . . . . . . . . . . . . . . . . . . . . . . . . . . . . 173

## Section 9—Allies, Advocates, and Co-conspirators: From the Inside Out . . . . . . . . . . . . . . . . . . . . . . . . . . . 175

Changing the Status Quo . . . . . . . . . . . . . . . . . . . . . . . . . 176

Many Feelings About Segregation . . . . . . . . . . . . . . . . . . 177

Someone Had To . . . . . . . . . . . . . . . . . . . . . . . . . . . . . . . . . 179

Flagpole Co-conspiracy . . . . . . . . . . . . . . . . . . . . . . . . . . . 180

Many Firsts . . . . . . . . . . . . . . . . . . . . . . . . . . . . . . . . . . . . . . 181

Sixty Years Ago . . . . . . . . . . . . . . . . . . . . . . . . . . . . . . 182
Standing on the Right Side of History. . . . . . . . . . . . . . . 184
More Love, Less Fear . . . . . . . . . . . . . . . . . . . . . . . . . . 185
We Shall Overcome. . . . . . . . . . . . . . . . . . . . . . . . . . . . 187

## Section 10—Good Trouble, Necessary Trouble: From the Inside Out . . . . . . . . . . . . . . . . . . . . . . . 189

Stand for Our Global Family . . . . . . . . . . . . . . . . . . . . . 190
Unbought and Unbossed . . . . . . . . . . . . . . . . . . . . . . 192
Good Samaritan. . . . . . . . . . . . . . . . . . . . . . . . . . . . . . 193
National Memorial for Peace and Justice . . . . . . . . . . . . . 194
Rest in Power. . . . . . . . . . . . . . . . . . . . . . . . . . . . . . . . 195
A Dream and a Call to Stay Woke . . . . . . . . . . . . . . . . . 196

## Section 11—Our Stories: From the Inside Out . . . . . 197

Black History *Is* American History . . . . . . . . . . . . . . . . . 198
And So It Began... . . . . . . . . . . . . . . . . . . . . . . . . . . . . 199
Trek Into Darkness . . . . . . . . . . . . . . . . . . . . . . . . . . . .200
A New Origin Story . . . . . . . . . . . . . . . . . . . . . . . . . . . 201
1619: Oneness Is Not Sameness. . . . . . . . . . . . . . . . . . .202
A Sinister Bet. . . . . . . . . . . . . . . . . . . . . . . . . . . . . . . .203
Jim Crow Code . . . . . . . . . . . . . . . . . . . . . . . . . . . . . .204
Oluale Kossola and Africatown . . . . . . . . . . . . . . . . . . .205
Spiritual and Genetic Siblings . . . . . . . . . . . . . . . . . . . .206
We Must Face Our Fear . . . . . . . . . . . . . . . . . . . . . . . .207
I'm Curious. Are You?. . . . . . . . . . . . . . . . . . . . . . . . . .209

**Section 12—Our Way Out of No Way:
From the Inside Out** ............................211

To the Degree We Become Conscious ................. 212

Seven Years ......................................... 213

Awareness Can Be Curative .......................... 214

Now Is the Time to Be Free ......................... 215

I Am *Every* Woman ................................. 216

In Pursuit of Freedom............................... 217

**Appendix A:**
Centers for Spiritual Living Vision Statement .......... 218

**Appendix B:**
CSL Declaration of Principles ....................... 219

**About the Author** ............................... 221

# Editor's Note

Throughout these pages, readers will encounter a number of synonyms for God, including Love, Life, the Divine, and Creative Principle, among others. All synonyms for God have an initial capital letter.

In addition to encompassing Rev. Dr. Andriette Earl's columns from *Science of Mind* magazine dating back to January 2012, this book also includes the Daily Guides she created for the February 2024 issue of the magazine. Readers will see twenty-seven Daily Guides within these pages. The two not included were incorporated into the author's Introduction.

For ease of reading, we shortened Ernest Holmes's name to Holmes in many instances. Any reference to Holmes should be read as meaning Ernest Holmes.

Within these pages, the author frequently refers to Centers for Spiritual Living (CSL) and the organization's Vision Statement and Declaration of Principles. Those can be found in the appendixes at the end of the book.

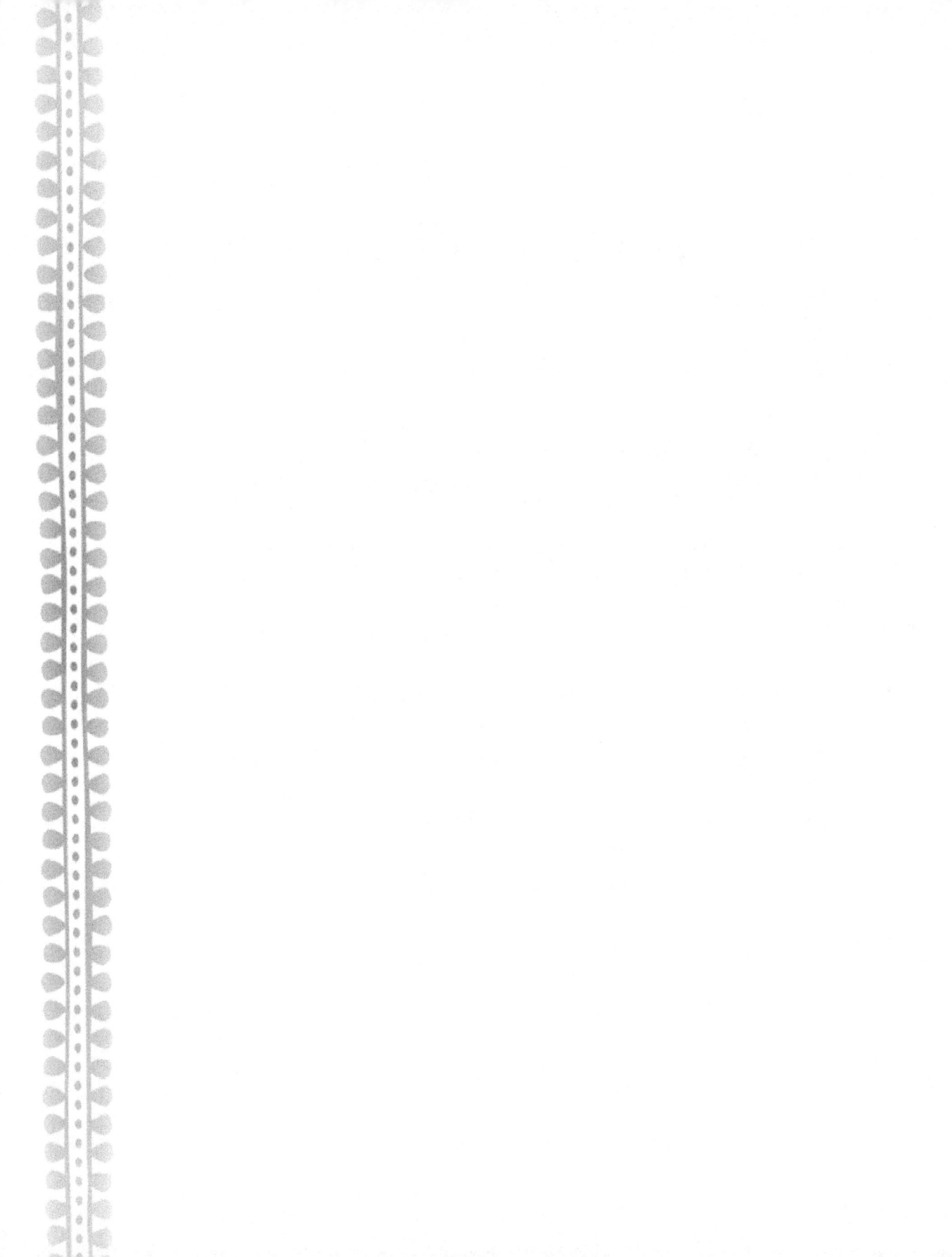

# Foreword

Wisdom and clarity, rooted in deep study and personal experience, are the gifts the Reverend Andriette Earl brings to so many in her expansive sphere of influence. I have been blessed to benefit from her counsel over the years. Long before she became an author, she was a confidant and spiritual guide to me. Still is. She is my beloved sister—support I can turn to when my wounds are fresh. The wisdom she shares with me, with other friends, and with many of us fellow travelers—her wisdom, her way—has been a balm along our circuitous, bumpy roads to self-discovery.

This book encapsulates the core of that profound wisdom. Her insight is concentrated here and brings us back home to our essential Self and the peace we long for in our over-scheduled lives and anxiety-ridden world. We have never needed the light of a new consciousness more than now.

*From the Inside Out* charts a course to a higher consciousness, a way of thinking that, with practice, brings our lives into balance and instills a lasting inner peace. Who doesn't yearn for relief from an over-scheduled, fast-changing, anxiety-ridden world? Rev. Andriette invites us to see that our challenges and our changes always coexist in divine order. A powerful storyteller, she shows us that no matter how painful our circumstances, each one calls us to grow in self-awareness and courage, to break through the barriers blocking our growth, to seek our soul's purpose. Our brilliant and elegant leader did just that.

Andriette Earl's insights here and in her stirring presentations change lives. They awaken in us the truth she wants us to hold and live with, in faith and courage: The power of God is limitless, and that power resides within us and as us. She teaches that we are human and divine, and that our divinity is innate and gives us dominion over our circumstances and our lives. *From the Inside Out* opens our hearts to this truth.

With this treasury of wisdom, you learn to trust and embrace your divinity and allow it to guide you toward living in ways that fulfill your soul's purpose. This is a book you will cherish. Steeped in spiritual principles, guided always by love, this book will open your heart to joy and your life to fulfilling your purpose.

— **Susan L. Taylor**
Founder and CEO,
National CARES Mentoring Movement;
Editor-in-Chief Emerita, *Essence Magazine*

# Introduction

*I believe every one of us is born with a purpose. No matter who you are, what you do, or how far you think you have to go, you have been tapped by a force greater than yourself to step into your God-given calling.*

—Oprah Winfrey

My entree to Science of Mind (SOM) came as I took classes with Rev. Terry Cole-Whittaker in 1982. I "met" her months earlier through her television program. She introduced me to affirmations, and I used them with immense success to shift my beliefs and circumstances. I began the class with skepticism, doubting the veracity of how she said *it* worked and the power of principle. Ever the dutiful student, I persevered, and commuted from San Francisco to San Diego to continue with Rev. Terry's instruction. My life was transforming, and I was smitten. This stuff worked!

Fast-forward thirty years. I am an ordained SOM minister, senior and founding minister of a thriving center, and a new columnist for *Science of Mind* magazine. When Judy Morley asked me to write a column, I assumed it would be for a year, maybe less. However, this book is a compilation of the monthly columns I have written for *Science of Mind* magazine continuously since 2012, and this book includes each of my columns through 2023.

In preparation for this book project, I began reviewing all the columns I had written. I anticipated discerning a consistent, well-defined, linear progression in my spiritual development over the past eleven years. I was surprised—and a bit disenchanted—to discover that was not so. My progression was simultaneously circuitous, inelegant, and public. As I reintroduced myself, for the first time in years, to the stories, observations, and reflections I shared, I was a bit embarrassed to realize I offered our readers so many repetitive themes.

Rather than forming a linear growth line, this collection emerges more tree-like—with branches emerging from a well-formed core, fashioned of my beliefs, values, and experiences—each branch born of and nurtured by my core, unconstrained and blossoming into an upward spiral of willingness, revealing my vulnerability, fallibility, and endurance. My authentic self. I was learning, revising, and unlearning as I wrote. I came to value my recurring themes for the healing opportunities they offered.

I was enormously grateful for the invitation to write the Daily Guides for the magazine's February 2024 issue, included in this book. I began this Black history project with great enthusiasm. I meditated, visioned, and then researched numerous well-known and several less well-known contributors to Black history. I even created a spreadsheet detailing the individuals, organizations, legislation, and historical events that resonated most with my vision. I had more than seventy options to consider. Every day of writing revealed even more options. I was overwhelmed by the possibilities and the need to choose twenty-nine.

Among the obvious possibilities were my all-time favorites. I had to include them. However, as I surrendered to this discovery process, I began to let go of my affinities and inclinations. I commenced writing what Spirit guided me to write.

My research and focus on the Black experience in America were often emotionally wrenching, like scraping a healing scab. I acknowledge feeling traumatized by the consistent reign of terror my ancestors experienced. I also was awed by their faith, courage, and perseverance. Moreover, I felt the weight of displaying my Black gaze, knowing most of our magazine's readers view Black history—American history—through a very different lens.

Similarly, I was surprised and uncomfortable when some of my Black history stories featured non-Black contributors. My heart knew they must be included; my mind was caught up in arithmetic, calculating how many fewer Black voices would be heard and stories told if I used these precious twenty-nine pages in this way. My heart embraced my mind and collaborated on loving, creative ways to be inclusive and help readers see themselves in these Guides.

This is a testament to how well prayer, visioning, and meditation work. In my case, the late Rep. John Lewis came through strong. I recalled that just months before his death, while on the Edmund Pettus Bridge during the 55th anniversary of Bloody Sunday, he said, "Speak up, speak out, get in the way. ... Get in good trouble, necessary trouble, and help redeem the soul of America."

I received and accepted my marching and writing orders from the *spirit* of Rep. Lewis. I got that I was to uplift some of the folks who committed and contributed to the highest and best for Black folks and fought for their civil rights. I was to center my attention on some of the folks who spoke up, spoke out, and got in the way; to issue a call to action and highlight those who engaged in "good trouble, necessary trouble," often at great personal and professional risk.

This is me speaking up and out. Ernest Holmes said, "Only when we speak *from* the heart do we speak *to* the heart." I am speaking from my heart, and it is liberating.

I also borrowed from Fannie Lou Hamer's wisdom, knowing her truth: "When I liberate myself, I liberate others. If you don't speak out ain't nobody going to speak out for you." I made peace with the fact that my reticence at inclusion could rob readers of much-needed clear examples and exemplary models of how anyone and everyone can participate and how so many can be allies. These few individuals model how to lead from love, commit to justice, and land on the side of right, all the while working to demonstrate a world that works for all—those who do not identify as Black and yet fully demonstrate loving allyship, active advocacy, and the courage of co-conspiracy in support of freedom and justice for all.

Dr. Martin Luther King Jr. alluded to this in speaking of what "good men" must do as co-conspirators. He wrote: "When evil men plot, good men must plan. When evil men burn and bomb, good men must build and bind. When evil men shout ugly words of hatred, good men must commit themselves to the glories of love. Where evil men would seek to perpetuate an unjust status quo, good men must seek to bring into being a real order of justice."

To paraphrase Holmes: Somehow, out of the depth of the universe, some great demand was made of me. I answered it in joy.

This collection of writings—created from the inside out—is my tree of life. It holds it all. Every branch, leaf, and blossom correspond to a point of growth, stagnation, trauma, and/or nurturance. It is not my speaker's voice—that's already fully established and flows easily, unlike my writing, in which I had not yet fully developed the confidence to brazenly carve my authenticity and vulnerabilities in the granite of print media. Even so, this book tracks my thawing from frozen fear and resistance to writing and sharing from the inside out. It has been therapeutic and often cathartic. My prayer is that these writings inspire deeper, more authentic interest, acceptance, and inclusion.

I have come to accept and embrace that my unique *Science of Mind* magazine trek was never meant to be the linear process I anticipated. Instead, its true intent was freedom. It worked. I released many of my doubts and fears. In this autumn of my life, I now trust inner guidance manifesting as my writing voice. I recognize and honor the metamorphosis of each of the branches, blossoms, and leaves in my tree of life. This project shook my tree to release everything no longer beneficial and coaxed me up and out on the branches, even as I tumbled off a few. I am grateful I never gave up and that I learned to let the dead branches and leaves continue to fall away.

This book comprises my affirmations and stories declaring the courage, faith, and love I perceive in others and choose to claim and express myself. Writing assisted me in more fully embracing my faith in God and setting my desired mental equivalents, about which Holmes said, "The range of our possibilities at the present time does not extend far beyond the range of our present concepts. As we bring ourselves to a greater vision, we induce a greater concept and thereby demonstrate more in our experience. In this way there is a continuous growth and unfoldment taking place." Exactly.

The initial drafts were for me alone, to help alleviate my paralysis and the anxiety of writing. Now, I offer this book to you, from my heart to yours, to read as you will. Perhaps you will begin reading from the beginning, or perhaps you will just allow it to open to a page where something speaks to you. Even if you begin from the back and work your way forward, your process is perfect. You cannot do it wrong. However you choose to read it is perfect—for you. Please explore whatever calls to you in this moment. The rest can wait for another day.

The door of the soul opens inward, so experience this from *the inside out*. Be open. Be willing. Be blessed.

— **Rev. Dr. Andriette Earl**
August 2024

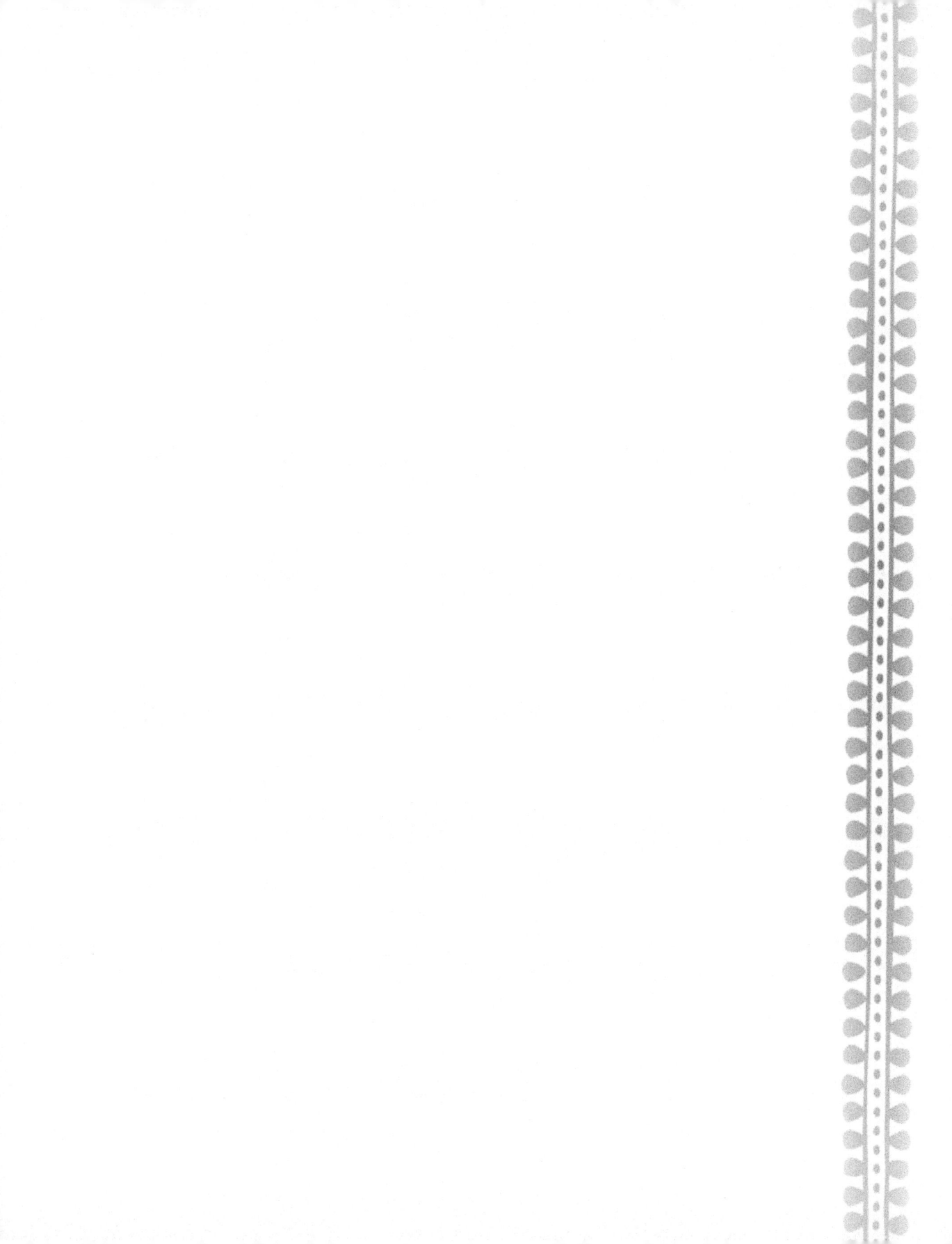

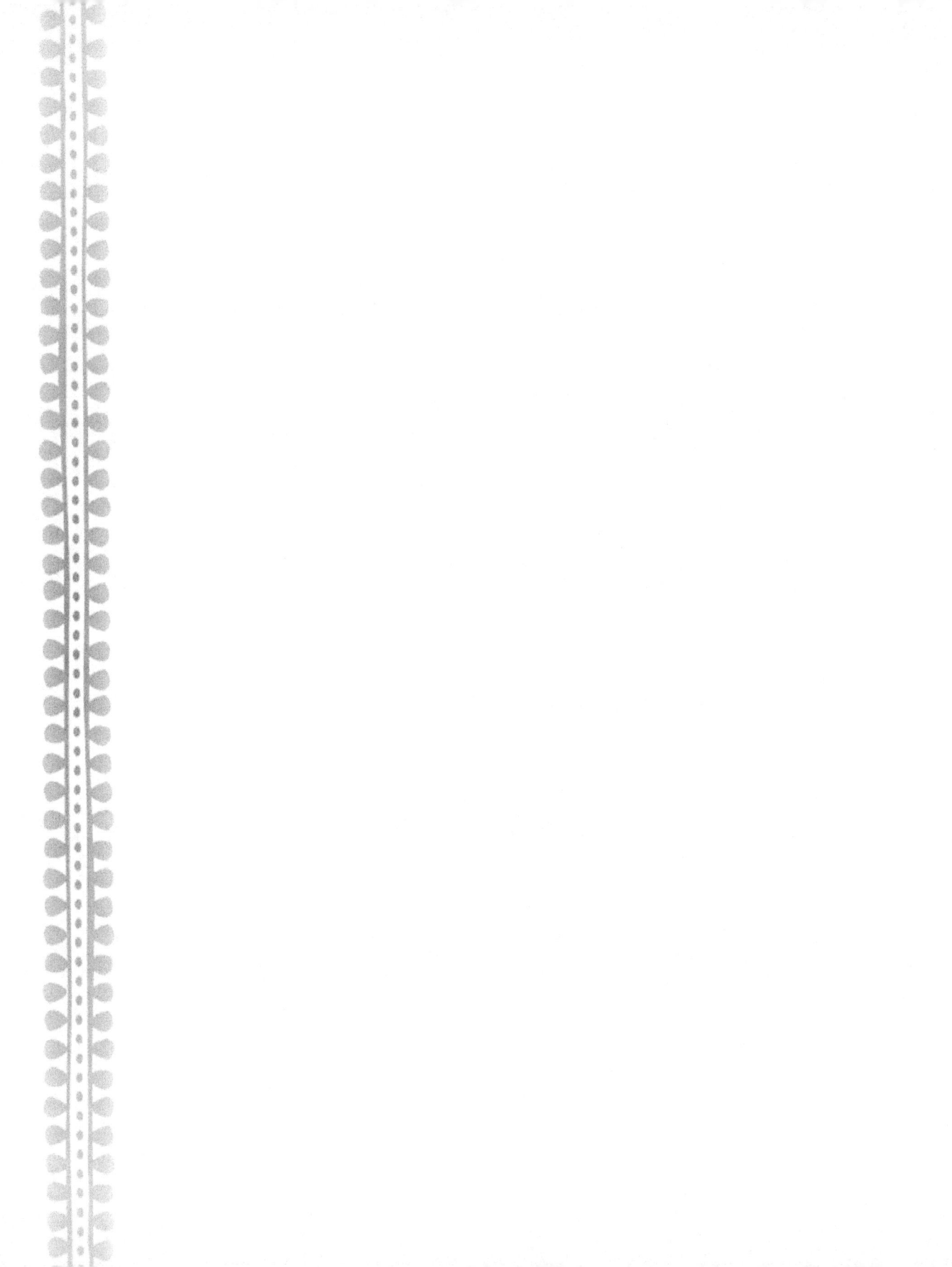

## SECTION ONE

# *Love*

## FROM THE INSIDE OUT

*Agape is something of the understanding, creative, redemptive goodwill for all men. It is a love that seeks nothing in return. It is an overflowing love; it's what theologians would call the love of God working in the lives of men. And when you rise to love on this level, you begin to love men, not because they are likeable, but because God loves them.*

— Rev. Dr. Martin Luther King Jr.

# Deeper in Love

We are called to love completely and unconditionally. Now, that's a high calling. There are always relationships where loving "them" is easy, and there are also those in which, well, we find it less easy to love. Our challenge is to love everyone more deeply, always.

Everyone and always seem to be at the core of this calling, and yet that is where we get hung up. Master teacher Jesus admonishes us to, "Love your enemies and bless the one who curse you. ... For if you love those who love you, what benefit is it to you?" (Matthew 5:44–46, Aramaic translation). I acknowledge that at first blush, I want to argue that to love those who love us is sufficient benefit unto itself, but then I realize that for our lives to become all they are intended to be, we must expand the circle of who we love. Jesus invites us into the center of the whole of life and its opportunities for authentic love and connection.

The celebrated R&B group The O'Jays croon:
> *Deeper in love, in love with you,*
> *Deeper in love with you*
> *With every step I make,*
> *With every breath I take*
> *...deeper in love with you.*

If only it were as easy as the chorus suggests to open our hearts fully without fear or doubt. And maybe it is—if we begin practicing on ourselves.

Ernest Holmes reminds us, "Divine Presence within me is everlasting Love. God in me does the loving, and I have no fear. ... I came into this world to love, and I am loving." To the degree that we embrace this as our individual truth and the purpose of our being as love, we can release our resistance to loving everyone, always. It begins with loving ourselves unconditionally and subsequently relating to each other with an expectancy of the highest and best for all concerned.

Love is the antidote for fear, doubt, and petty disagreements. I can sense the possibilities, the transformation of the planet, beginning with each of us shifting into deeper love right where we are now.

—*Published in the March 2012* Science of Mind *magazine*

# PARTNERS

*The Spirit is both an over-dwelling and an indwelling Presence.
We are immersed in It, and It flows through us as our very life. ...
Nothing could be more intimate than the personal relationship
between the individual and that Divine Presence that is both
the Center and the Source of each person's being.*

— Ernest Holmes

I grew up hearing folks say that we are "God's hands." Yet, if I were to anthropomorphize God, I would declare us the heart of Its being. Our interaction with one another is one of the ways we express the love of God. It's as if we are in partnership with God, at work to support each other in our growth and development. Spirit supports us in all we do. Spirit provides everything required for our life's journey, and we always have sufficient support to be our best. All people, things, places, and situations are for us. They may not look, feel, or behave in the way we expect or appreciate, and yet, they are still here in support of our divine evolution. Yes, even if it felt like betrayal and looked like abandonment, there is still that which we can call forth: our greatest-yet-to-be.

Iyanla Vanzant, our wise and witty sister, reminds us that each of our relationships serves us for a reason, a season, or a lifetime. She helps elucidate Bishop T. D. Jakes's metaphor that people serve us like scaffolding does a builder: They play an essential role in our lives until "the building is built," and then they are removed because the project no longer requires scaffolding. No one is to blame for their leaving; they have completed their service. It's all in divine order.

When I ask myself, "What has this come to teach me?", and then listen to discern the gift in my challenging experience, I find myself often amazed and always blessed by what the experience reveals. The answers are within and await our inquiry. Through authentic exploration, we gain essential insight into how everything serves us. Life—yours and mine—continuously unfolds in divine order, and we can count on support from our partners.

—*Published in the September 2012* Science of Mind *magazine*

# Human AND Divine

In our perception of the world and our own little corners, we yearn to up-level our collective expression of *human*. We desperately want us all to be, as Howard Thurman suggested, "more loving in my heart." The phrase suggests that we must begin this transformation from the inside out. When we seek evidence of our humanity, do we embrace our loving compassionate nature, perceiving ourselves as the Good Samaritan in the Gospel of Luke? In seeking evidence of our divinity, do we perceive our light as shining bright and basking in the synchronicity of the flow of the *All* Good? My sense is not so much, at least not most of the time.

We engage the creative process when we set an intention for our head (thinking) and heart (feeling nature) to align in oneness and synchronicity. Many of us have come to embrace that we truly are both human and divine, and yet we struggle. Imagine if we practiced expanding our sense of humanity so it developed to be in perfect sync with the highest sense of our divinity. This would truly be a marriage made in heaven—a mystical marriage.

*Marriage*, as an expression of empowered partnership, also is an agreement, a union. It includes compromise; it means creating something that honors each individual entity and yet nurtures the intention and vision to manifest through collaboration. Marriage requires continuous growth and the intentional alignment of both parties in order to progress and prosper.

In mystical marriage, not unlike physical marriage, an "I do" consciousness and intention ushers in "We do!" and an expanded sense of oneness, unconditional love, commitment, and compassion. Our desire to wed our humanness to our divinity and then to emerge less limited and more divinely inspired happens through this bond. It's on the wings of love, through expressions of unconditional love and acceptance of what is, that we release the fear of what we might lose and realize that we stand to gain new life.

—*Published in the June 2013* Science of Mind *magazine*

# *You Had It All the Time*

*When you do not bring forward what is within you,
what is within you will destroy you. But when you bring forth
what is within you, what is within you will heal and save you.*

— Gnostic Gospel of St. Thomas

The jarring, prying question, "Just who do you think you are?", is a virtual pop quiz. The answers reveal personal truth—how we see the self. Some of us know who we are and have the temerity to declare this truth outright. Some know who they are but never could declare it out loud. Some have based their self-awareness on others' perceptions of them. Sadly, some of us have mastered ignoring our divinity for so long that we rendered ourselves dumb in response.

Bless our hearts. The truth is, God is all there is; we are all divine beings. This is the truth that sets us free (as referred to in John 8:32).

We are undefeatable. It's who we are. We have had and will continue to have challenges that either launch us to unimaginable heights or snatch the bottom out from under us. The key to living our highest visions lies within. Success is wholly in our minds and mouths, as our thoughts and words. Implanted in all of us before time began were the dominion and the power to transform our circumstances. As soon as we accept responsibility for this divine bequest and learn to trust ourselves, we can more fully let go and let God.

As prodigal sons and daughters, it is time for us to wake up and claim our divine birthright. Our full inheritance awaits us. Honor the self and begin to live more consistently in alignment with Infinite Presence—in oneness.

The infinite love, grace, and guidance we yearn for have always been and are available to us now. "Deep within our hearts, each of us knows the truth," Alan Cohen reminds us. "The spirit within you is greater than anything in the outer world. The power of your life is now returned to your own hands, where it has always been. You had it all the time."

—*Published in the October 2013* Science of Mind *magazine*

# The Heart of the Matter

*What you do speaks so loudly that I cannot hear what you say.*

— Ralph Waldo Emerson

Our love and intent are causal. Our ultimate experience is the collective effect of *our* intent, consciousness, and behavior. We have the wherewithal and power to affect a greater impact on our world than many of us honor. We can begin by choosing to go deeper into our motivations and decisions about our individual lives and the environment of our global body temple, Mother Earth.

This may be more easily recognized in our individual life experiences. For example, I know someone who, more than a decade ago, experienced a cluster of heart arrhythmia incidents. They were at once painful, debilitating, and frightening. She felt relieved when doctors found no cause. During a subsequent incident, she was hospitalized, and that got her attention. She realized she could either buy into a cycle of fear or she could pray, "in faith believing" her cure would come.

She ultimately found her voice, bargained for time to meditate and pray, and declared that her condition could and would shift without defibrillator paddles or drugs. And it did. However, she never got to the actual heart of the matter. She chose not to look deeper and discern the cause. She simply became adept at managing subsequent episodes. She ignored the common sense approach to honoring, caring for, and enhancing her sole body temple. With her focus remaining on the effect, she essentially suspended her wisdom and awareness that there is always a cause to every effect.

I sense a corollary between our individual body and the manifest global body of our affairs. By right of consciousness, our collective cities, countries, and planet are our global body temple, the manifest consequence of our consciousness. We will reveal a world that works for all when we, as conscious inhabitants, take full responsibility for fostering this temple's optimum condition and operation. It is time for us to join in support of the committed and begin mitigating any harm we have caused each other and to our own global body temple. We must get to the heart of the matter.

—*Published in the January 2013* Science of Mind *magazine*

# Celebrating Our History

*My activism did not spring from being black. ... Racial injustice ...
was a challenge to my belief in the oneness of the human family.*

— Bayard Rustin, in a letter dated April 1986

August 2013 was the fiftieth anniversary of the Civil Rights Movement. The turbulence and violence of 1963 claimed many Black and White activists. As a pre-teen then, I marveled at the consciousness and courage of activists like Dr. King and Bayard Rustin, who dedicated their lives to advancing civil rights and justice.

Until President Obama posthumously awarded Rustin the Medal of Freedom, the legacy of this brilliant organizer went largely unknown. Born a Quaker, he was the activist who not only mentored Dr. King in the principles of nonviolent noncooperation but also was the chief architect of the 1963 March on Washington and organizer of the first Freedom Rides in 1947.

Because Rustin was openly gay, he was forced to work behind the scenes, as his sexuality was the target of attacks by those opposed to the civil rights of others.

Through it all, he taught and authentically practiced unconditional love. Rustin said, "When I say I love [Mississippi Senator James] Eastland, it sounds preposterous—a man who brutalizes people. But you love him, or you wouldn't be here. You're going to Mississippi to create social change—and you love Eastland in your desire to create conditions that will redeem his children. Loving your enemy is manifest in putting your arms not around the man but around the social situation, to take power from those who misuse it—at which point they can become human, too." He expressed the true heart of humanity.

His message of unconditional love is essential for such a time as this. It is up to us to learn our history, tell the truth, and pay homage accordingly. Even now, fifty years later, history still ekes out the names of those who stood resolute for human rights and justice for all, often sacrificing their lives for our greater good. It's up to us to celebrate our authentic collective history and be the loving heart of humanity.

—*Published in the February 2014* Science of Mind *magazine*

# Daily Resurrection

I am grateful for the arrival of spring. This past winter presented death, well beyond the seasonal metaphors. We were visited by homicides, grand juries, questions of prosecutorial ethics, protests, and tear gas.

Now that the almanac declares spring, my personal spring is fertile and has begun to sprout hope in the very midst of bloodshed, litigation, marches, doubts, and fear.

I needed and sought the newness of spring and the "glad surprise" written about by Dr. Howard Thurman: "[It] comes at the end of a long total tragedy and tribulation. It is as if a man stumbling in the darkness, having lost his way, finds that the spot at which he falls is the foot of the stairway that leads from darkness into light. Such is the glad surprise. This is what Easter means in the experience of the race. This is the resurrection! It is the announcement that life cannot ultimately be conquered by death."

I learned from *A Course in Miracles* that resurrection is denying the power of death and instead affirming love and the eternal sanctity of all life.

Resurrection requires surrender. Rev. Dr. Michael Bernard Beckwith says, "Surrender is not giving in to the negativity of life but rather yielding to the greatest possibility of life."

When we consistently focus more on Infinite Possibility than on the disappointments of our past or limit ourselves by finite facts, we surrender and are certain to awaken, transcend, and rise to meet our true self.

In surrender, we resurrect daily. We need not wait for any particular season. As we surrender our lower self—which may be attached or even addicted to doubt, despair, worry, fear, conflict, and chaos—we simultaneously rise above the lesser and engage the higher.

In this way, we weave divine love into the fabric of our lives. It lightens our burdens and, naturally, we rise. We can declare a fresh start—a new life—in which love triumphs over hate, grace neutralizes pain, and forgiveness transmutes the past.

Let us place a demand on divine love and call forth our resurrection.

—Published in the April 2015 Science of Mind *magazine*

## It Will Be Ours

I am moved by Burt Bacharach's lyrics, "What the world needs now is love." However, I do not believe, as he said, "That's the only thing that there's just too little of." There is definitely too little forgiveness, compassion, empathy, social and criminal justice, commitment to reconciliation, inclusion, acceptance, protection for "protected classes," respect for elders and youth, political freedom, justice, to name but a few.

Yet, I still rejoice in this simple perception, this empowered lyric, and this straight-forward declaration of what is ours to be and do in calling forth the world we want—love. A world that works for everyone? What exactly is the world we want?

When we view our requirements and preferences through our empathetic lenses, we recognize that we all desire the same and similar for ourselves and our beloveds. We just have not yet expanded our vision and dreams to include those we perceive as "other."

None of what we think is required for a world that works for everyone is even possible without demonstrating love. We are love, and when we express love with the fullness of our being, we also reveal the more being required of us.

During the 2015 Academy Awards ceremonies, "Glory" won the Oscar for Best Original Song. The co-composers, John Legend and Common, used their acceptance speech to remind us that although the movie *Selma* depicted history, its themes still bind us today.

In an interview, Legend said he identifies with Common's statement, "Love is all that is needed," to the extent that ending racism is about people being able to see "each other's humanity and learning to love each other."

Legend said, "I think it's not enough for us to extend the hand of love. It's important also that we look at policies we need to change as well."

Yes! What the world needs now is love and conscious acts of love. According to the Oscar-winning song:

> *One day, when the glory comes*
> *It will be ours, it will be ours.*
> *Oh, one day, when the war is won,*

*We will be sure, we will be here sure.*
*Oh glory, glory.*
*It will be ours—a world that works for everyone.*

—Published in the August 2015 Science of Mind *magazine*

# Joy Cometh in the Morning

*Weeping may tarry for the night, but joy cometh in the morning.*
— Psalm 30:5

There was a time when I wondered if "joy comes in the morning" was actually meant to be "joy comes in the mourning."

I can offer testimony that my most challenging experiences continue to inspire me beyond settling, and they assist me in clarifying my heart's true desire.

The view from the valley can be frightening, even paralyzing for some. Immersed in the dark of night, our weeping, sadness, and doubt appear to be who we are, not just our experience in the moment. In the morning, however, light floods in, and we are better able to discern the solutions hidden in the darkness. Just like the gospel lyrics fashioned from Psalm 30, we come to realize that "trouble don't last always." Praise God!

Isaiah 61:3 invites us to stand in our transformative power and up-level our response to life's challenges: "Give beauty for ashes, joy for mourning, praise for the spirit of heaviness."

The key is to shift our attention from the valley of negative perception and defeating predictions and focus on a mountaintop experience—what we truly want, what we would truly love.

We give beauty for ashes when we focus our attention on what we would love rather than being resigned to facts as they appear.

We give joy for mourning when we embrace a joyous attitude while experiencing troubling circumstances.

We give praise for the spirit of heaviness when we sustain an attitude of gratitude rather than capitulate into gloom or a sense of hopelessness.

For the past several months, I have been challenging myself to respond to life from the inner inquiry, "What would I love?" This shift requires that I engage and control my imagination. Our intention is not to avoid life; it is to live in alignment with our highest vision so we feel joy pouring in and over our experience.

How much joy are we willing to accept (in the morning)?

*—Published in the September 2015* Science of Mind *magazine*

# Keys to the Kingdom

*There is a key to right living, a golden key to happiness and success,
and this key is in our own thought; it is our affirmative prayer.*

— Ernest Holmes

When I attended my first Science of Mind classes, I found the teaching implausible. I was in my 30s and convinced that I knew everything, certainly much more than I do now. I was doubtful that I (or anyone like me) had direct access to power and the ability to truly transform life. I accepted the initial lessons as a personal challenge, engaged faith, committed to practice, and endeavored to prove the principles in my life. One of the greatest gifts I received is the awareness that not only do I have more power than I thought, I am *empowered*. It was as if I had been given the keys to the kingdom.

One key is to believe—to *know*—and to speak from this certainty. It may sound simple; however, it is not easy. Our lives are full to overflowing with a variety of challenges and opportunities to expand our sense of self. Too often, when challenged, we err by entertaining our doubts and nurturing our self-loathing.

Therefore, the second key must be to remember the first key. We must engage our faith and consistently remind ourselves that we are capable of expanding and then see ourselves living beyond our current experience or perceived limit.

There is also a powerful key at the core of the Nazarene's profound teaching and love practice that can be synthesized as, "It is done unto you as you believe."

This awareness of how life evolves is crucial to initiating a sustainable positive shift in our lives. Jesus's brand of unconditional love ensured he is not dependent on, restricted by, or distracted by personalities and could instead fully engage spiritual principle through his own thought.

His legacy of love is an essential key and offers us a huge clue about what is required. As in scripture when he admonished his followers to "love your neighbor as yourself," this may be the key we misplace most often. The good news is this golden key can be readily retrieved, as it is written on our hearts.

—*Published in the June 2017* Science of Mind *magazine*

# Solid as a Rock

*He is like a man who built a house and he dug and he went deep and laid the foundation on the rock, and when there was a flood, the flood beat on that house and it could not shake it, for its foundation was founded on the rock.*

— Luke 6:48

I was born and raised in the greater San Francisco Bay Area, known to many as "earthquake country." Living near several fault lines, we were encouraged to be prepared for the inevitable earthquake. Some heeded this advice, and some did not, although the catastrophic 1989 earthquake got our full attention. Many of us purchased or created earthquake preparedness kits. I even went to the effort and expense of having my house bolted to the foundation so that it could not slide during a major earthquake.

What the contractor did at my house was akin to digging "deep and laying the foundation on the rock," cited in the gospel of Luke. This same principle clarifies the relationship of a tree's roots to its potential height and stability: The deeper the roots, the higher the tree can grow.

This notion of digging deep can be similarly applied to our intention to stand stable in the face of challenges. However, it is not enough just to dig deep.

The depth of our connection must be to a truly stabilizing force. This is in contrast to those buildings in the greater Bay Area that were built on landfills and destined to be rendered unsteady. It is the same with us.

We are called to dig deep by trusting love and tying our lives and dreams to perfect God, perfect human, and perfect being. Form everything from this truth. Our every musing, thought, dream, and prayer all are tied securely to the truth of our being, which is our oneness and divinity.

Borrowing from an old hymn, I declare on our behalf: We rely on nothing less than divine principle, the solid rock, on which we stand. "All other ground is sinking sand."

—Published in the January 2018 *Science of Mind* magazine

# I Pray Love

*The country is in deep trouble. We've forgotten that a rich life consists fundamentally of serving others, trying to leave the world a little better than you found it. We need the courage to question the powers that be, the courage to be impatient with evil and patient with people, the courage to fight for social justice. In many instances, we will be stepping out on nothing and just hoping to land on something. But that's the struggle. To live is to wrestle with despair, yet never allow despair to have the last word.*

— Dr. Cornel West

The 2018 midterm elections received more attention and scrutiny than any in recent history. Print media, on-air pundits, and online bloggers seemed insatiable in their coverage. Many of us jumped directly into the conflict and fray. One of my ministerial colleagues, Rev. Karen Langford, took a different approach and wrote a collective consciousness prayer.

Honoring the immense power of affirmative prayer, I was inspired to adapt it to my vision and voice.

In gratitude for her inspiration and in abiding faith, I declare:

I pray for our U.S. government that it honors and reflects our nation's diversity, that it be high functioning, and that it be committed to justice and inclusive outcomes toward a world that works for everyone.

I pray for our members of Congress that they work in harmony toward the highest and best for all Americans.

I pray for the president of our country that he embraces and engages the whole, perfect, and complete nature of each and every person, organization, and country.

I pray for my fellow U.S. citizens that we live in peace and harmony, that we honor and experience each other through love and inclusion, with compassion and in acceptance of our diversity.

I pray for all people everywhere that we live in peace and harmony.

I pray we recognize and realize our oneness, that we live in unity, and honor our diversity as members of our amazing human race.

I pray love with "liberty and justice for all," and as Dr. Cornel West said, that we "never forget that justice is what love looks like in public."

And so it is.

*—Published in the February 2019* Science of Mind *magazine*

# Love's in Need of Love

*If love and peace you treasure*
*Then you'll hear me when I say*
*Love's in need of love today*
*Don't delay, send yours in right away*
*Hate's goin' 'round, breaking many hearts*
*Stop it please, before it's gone too far.*

— Stevie Wonder

I often cry when I hear Stevie Wonder's "Love's in Need of Love Today." (The truth is, on occasions, I actually have wept.) It's a beautiful song, and every listening leaves me with so much to unpack.

Wonder's musical genius and unabashed declaration that love is in need of love is both a creative lyric and wordplay on truth. It pierces the tender center of my heart every time I listen to it. Am I the only one left questioning:

- Is my love in need of love?

- How often am I actualizing love?

- Is the love I profess backed by more than my words?

The song was released in 1976, yet Wonder's lyrical admonishment that we must stop coming up love-short before "it's gone too far" is an essential message for such a time as this. So I ask you, how far is too far when it comes to love? T. S. Eliot reminds us, "Only those who will risk going too far can possibly find out how far one can go."

Many have already experienced our hearts guiding us to places our minds did not yet want to go. Still living in the effect of fear and doubt, too often we have tried to remain indifferent, and in so doing, we withheld love.

I pray we have learned from those times and realize our heart knows best and always beckons us to love more deeply than we thought we could. The thing is, our heart alway guides us to ever-increasing expressions of love. It knows that more love—not apathy or rejection—is required of each of us in every situation and circumstance.

As Wonder sings, "We all must take precautionary measures." Family, our challenge today is let us endeavor to see how much further we can go with love. It's time for us to send our love in, right away. Don't delay.

*—Published in the May 2020* Science of Mind *magazine*

# A New Heaven

*And I saw new Heavens and a new Earth,
the former Heavens and the former Earth had departed.*

— Book of Revelation 21:1

The health and well-being of our society, planet, and life itself are simply the manifestation of our consciousness. I believe love is a dynamic healing power and actually the path to our collective well-being. Love is a life-promoting, energetic, healing frequency, and at this level of consciousness, we readily experience miracles. So why does it appear otherwise?

The answer is simple: There is a crack in our foundation. An intentional review of American history reveals a crack of tribalism—separation, exclusion, and otherness—intentionally created and framed into the original construct and subsequent renovations of our basic foundation. This experiment in democratic systems of order, access, and protection was structured and erected on a severely cracked foundation.

This crack is especially apparent in our experience of "energetic hysteria," living in twin pandemics of systemic racism and Covid-19. As challenging and painful as the pandemics are, I find great solace in Dr. Ernest Holmes's wisdom that "principle is not bound by precedent. ... We should confidently expect a greater good than we have ever experienced or than we have ever known of anyone experiencing."

I am relieved to be reminded that no matter how long or how out of alignment with our stated intention of inclusion and integrity, we can still rise to expect and manifest our greater good.

Any real change requires a shift in our thinking and our actions. Every cell in our body and the body of our affairs is affected by consciousness—our awareness of what really is happening—and how we respond. Because our individual consciousness and positive energy manifest as our common unity, it behooves us to assess our generational beliefs and behaviors, adjust our current thinking, release our sacred cows, and relinquish any investment in exclusion.

If we are committed to living in a new world as our new normal, we must envision, embrace, and become the vibrational equivalent—the corresponding new heaven, as required, to beget our new Earth.

I give thanks in advance.

*—Published in the October 2020* Science of Mind *magazine*

# Magnetize Infinite Possibility

As we close the first quarter of 2021, many of us find ourselves still analyzing and ruminating on 2020. We are trying to discern what happened. What happened to our plans and vision? What happened to our family? What happened to and in our relationships? What happened to our work and how we work?

My prayer is that our questions assist us in being open to new and greater possibilities for all of us. We must not allow circumstances to distract us from or interfere with our intention, resolve, and vision. I am aware of the challenge of magnetizing and living fully in new possibilities. Even so, it is ours to be and do.

No matter who we are, we always live in the possibilities we believe are available to us. It truly is "done unto us as we believe," and this is what we express and experience. Even though we judge by appearances and are often inconsistent in embracing new possibilities and making the required changes to ensure them, we can change.

Opening ourselves to new possibilities requires us to evolve our belief systems and engage new stories and practices. We must change our thinking and feeling to magnetize the new. New Thought luminaries Ernest Holmes and Raymond Charles Barker believed that our future is not dependent on our past. This awareness, if we accept and embrace it, is golden. It's our get-out-of-jail-free card. It establishes that we are not as conditioned or limited as we might think by our past experiences. We can change, and our attention is best focused on this intention, even when it feels impossible.

Evolving our consciousness is the key to transmuting the impossible to the possible. Each of us accomplishes things we once deemed impossible, which first evolved to possible and then into our manifest experience. Remember this, and do not allow the past or the appearance of the impossible to deter you.

Infinite possibility surrounds us. When we tune in, divine love guides us to it and to our best outcomes. As we come into greater realization of divine life, limitless possibilities for 2021 reveal themselves.

Our good is always at hand. Magnetize it.

—*Published in the March 2021* Science of Mind *magazine*

# Trusting Truth

*Never let anything cause you to doubt your ability to demonstrate the Truth. Conceive of your word as being the Thing.*

— Ernest Holmes

My initial focus on my journey of becoming was to manifest more stuff, believing that would make my life complete. I had no clue that my true heart's desire was to demonstrate a deeper self-love. Who knew that a material wishlist would morph into my clear intention to unconditionally love, fully accept, and forgive myself? I had so much to learn.

One of the first lessons was to trust Divine Source, believe in my worthiness, know I am loved, and declare this truth with certainty. This was radical thinking at the time. I began to fashion affirmations declaring my highest and best. I recited these affirmations to develop and nurture my budding ideas into an empowering belief system.

My timing was spot on. This spiritual practice of trusting and affirming my divine good brought me out of deep depression—initially brightening my day, eventually my weeks, and ultimately my life. I learned to believe in my divinity, write statements affirming my best life, and declare this truth daily with enthusiasm and conviction.

That was forty years ago, and my journey of becoming continues. As we bring 2021 to closure, I acknowledge the extreme challenges this year wrought—challenges evident in global events, the multi-pandemics of the past two years, and our responses to it all.

Our world is on a journey of becoming, and so are we. I believe this journey guides us into greater awareness of who and how we are and can be, especially with and for each other. The journey draws us into an even higher vibration of love, grace, and connection. Whatever has happened or is happening now, truth is our navigator. We are here to trust the truth and make a difference.

Our intentional word is powerful. There is truth for us to demonstrate. Please join me in affirming this: "I engage Divine Mind and realize the best ways and means to call forth divine love so that harmony, peace, cooperation, unity, and mutual helpfulness are experienced by all."

—*Published in the December 2021* Science of Mind *magazine*

## We're in this Love Together

For more than a year, my early morning walks around Lake Merritt aided in opening my heart to spontaneous human connection. As a bonafide introvert, I am awed by having created an informal and joyous community among my fellow lake-walkers.

My walking buddy and I experience pleasant connections with several of the other walkers. Because we do not know their given names, we assigned nicknames to several regulars: Mack Caddy, Angela's Cousin, The Whisperer, Tall Baller, etc. We miss them when we do not see them, and we give and receive a hearty welcome when we reconnect.

This improbable sense of community revealed itself recently when an infestation of red algae in our beloved lake killed the fish, and many of the regular walkers stayed away or altered their routes. I was surprised that I missed the sense of togetherness and joyful, albeit brief, connection I embraced before this crisis. Unbeknownst to me, we had become a loosely knit community of early morning lake-walkers.

There was already an unspoken agreement on our behavior for letting runners and bikers pass and how to give way to the dogs and their people, all the while avoiding birds and their droppings. It is a valued gift that I can move through my community with the freedom and ease of my own pace. The algae infestation, resultant dead fish, and the upset to the bird population seemed to solidify our connection and set up an odd bonding experience.

When I began walking, I behaved as a true introvert. I spoke to other walkers and runners in my mind, never audibly. Over time, I feel more comfortable—safer—and I now make eye contact and greet them aloud. For me, this is connection. I am grateful I created this divine experience, and I fully acknowledge that this sense of lake community exists only in my mind and heart. This is where all sense of community is born.

I started walking the lake for my own health and well-being, and I have come to experience what Ernest Holmes described: "Love is the greatest healing power in the universe and the only thing that binds people together in a community of spirit."

—*Published in the December 2022* Science of Mind *magazine*

# *Bravely Live Your Divine Truth*

*No one else can live your truth. If you are yourself as honestly, authentically, and unapologetically as possible, that makes space for others to do the same thing.*

— Jessamyn Stanley

In our shared culture, being different seems increasingly dangerous. The erroneous idea that being mean, offensive, critical, and judgmental is being authentic has run amok. Cyberbullying is a thing and an opportunity to spew vitriol and remain anonymous in the crowd. Some do not survive these attacks. "I'm just being authentic," we say in our defense, while tucking our bloody sickles behind our backs.

I recently stumbled on to Jessamyn Stanley's blog. She shares her pain of not belonging and how it eroded her sense of self. Stanley, a self-described "fat, Black, queer woman," now stands brazenly for herself and all of us who look, sound, and live "different" in this public forum. She acknowledges the trolls and vitriol, and she affirms, "It's all about what you think you deserve. And no one can make you believe you deserve what you're worth if you don't think you deserve it."

Stanley managed to cultivate and nurture her authenticity on social media. She illuminates that in cultivating our authenticity, we cultivate divine love, embracing ourselves in compassion and truth. She offers us an invitation to intentionally expand our consciousness to accept the highest and best in all of us and endeavor to cultivate our highest vision for the divine beings we are. This requires us to be deliberate in our intention to cultivate and live our most authentic lives.

Saying *divine authenticity* feels redundant and yet essential to clarify the source and quality of our authenticity. Our philosophy teaches and reminds us that the Creator and all of us are one. Each of us is already whole, perfect, and complete. We must continue to cultivate our awareness of and practice this truth by releasing our fears, making loving choices, and envisioning positive outcomes.

We have all we need to cultivate and express our authenticity; our divine inheritance is ours to claim. Let's claim it, now.

—Published in the March 2023 Science of Mind *magazine*

# The Courage To Be Vulnerable

A year ago, I began supporting my beloved elder who has dementia. Recently, my life turned upside down when she suffered an acute stroke, leaving her entire left side paralyzed and compromising her ability to speak and swallow. She is now in hospice.

This is hard! My love for her is and always has been real. This is a vulnerable time for both of us. Both of us are off our game. We both are challenged in accepting what is. My work is to embrace this major change, even as she resists and I grieve. The pain challenges me to be vulnerable, to continue to recognize, embrace, and honor oneness and divine order. I am laid bare in this, my fears fully exposed.

I am facing my fears and acknowledging my need for self-care. Most of all, I miss belonging—the assured love connection we shared for more than 70 years. In this new iteration of our relationship, we are both fragile, jerked from the familiarity of our established relationship and obliged to surrender our false sense of control. Everything changed and all felt at risk.

The risks seem enormous. One perceived risk lies in acknowledging my deep love and co-abiding fear of loss through her impending transition. I weep in this awareness. My futile attempts to shield myself from the inevitable wounds in attending this phase of life and negotiating the universal stages of grief also pose a risk.

I truly am grateful that the benefits and gifts are even greater. Choosing to be vulnerable, I hold open my wounded heart. And risking increased pain, I instead experience an even greater love, more self-acceptance, and deeper peace.

Brené Brown's words offer a much-needed salve for my wounds: "Vulnerability is not winning or losing; it's having the courage to show up and be seen when we have no control over the outcome. Vulnerability is not weakness; it's our greatest measure of courage."

Though I often feel weak and ill prepared to execute this experience with the love, skill, and grace I desire, I affirm I have the courage to be vulnerable, accept the risks and love through my fears. I am grateful.

*—Published in the April 2023* Science of Mind *magazine*

SECTION 2

# Faith

## FROM THE INSIDE OUT

*Faith sees the invisible, believes the unbelievable,
and receives the impossible.*

—Corrie ten Boom

# What Are You Doing for Others?

*Life's most persistent and urgent question is: What are you doing for others?*

— Dr. Martin Luther King Jr.

Our spiritual community lovingly embraces and admires Harriet Tubman as our *spiritual* icon. Reverently called Black Moses, she was a woman of courage, compassion, and spiritual insight. Mother Harriet escaped slavery in 1849 and repeatedly risked torture by returning to free more than three hundred enslaved men, women, and children. She also served as a nurse and Union spy during the Civil War. She trusted God and was led by the spiritual guidance she received in dreams and visions.

Mother Harriet is a model whose life demonstrates that anyone can step up and step out to make a difference in his or her own life and in the lives of others.

I challenge myself to imagine what was required of her to (a) stand boldly in the face of mental and physical torture, (b) proceed to design, develop, and implement a strategy to steal away to a location unknown to her conscious mind, and then (c) return numerous times to successfully guide other captives to freedom. *What! How?* Most often, I cannot fathom her circumstances and frequently find myself reduced to tears. I'm never sure whether my tears are from my compassion for her challenges or judgment of my own reluctance to live in courage and compassion.

Mother Harriet's life of remarkable service parlayed human degradation and suffering into love, compassion, and faith. She embodies the compassionate heart eloquently expressed by Howard Thurman: "Keep open the door of thy heart. It matters not how many doors are closed against thee."

During February, America celebrates Black History. I am honored to lift up my shero, Harriet Tubman, this month and always as a guiding light of faith, love, compassion, and courage. She exemplifies that what was possible for her is possible for all.

— *Published in the February 2013* Science of Mind *magazine*

# BE WHOLE

John 5 recounts one of my favorite Bible stories. Jesus sees a *certain* invalid, a man, lying by the pool at Bethesda, and, "Knowing that he had been there a long time, he asked him, 'Wouldst thou be made whole?' Jesus then declared, 'Arise, take up thy bed, and walk.' And straightaway, the man was made whole and took up his bed and walked." This story illuminates that truth known and declared in faith removes the veil of effect and nullifies the past as prelude.

Can realizing our wholeness be that simple and immediate?

Wholeness is a choice. We must choose to see and experience ourselves as enough, exactly as we are now. The basis of our spiritual healing exists in rediscovering truth and full engagement in life. According to Ernest Holmes, "If one would take time, once a day at least, to let go of all that is not true and lay hold of reality; let go of doubt, distrust, worry, condemnation, and fear, and lay hold of Life in Its expressions of beauty, truth, and wholeness, mental congestion would be healed." Therefore, it is not magic; it is intentionality.

To "lay hold of reality," we must exercise our free will and choose and embrace our whole, perfect, and complete nature—our oneness. When we acknowledge and honor our spiritual wholeness, we experience being one with Life. No more duality; no good and bad. As we recognize the divine connection and continuity of Spirit and embrace all seeming opposites without judgment, we are one and whole.

The law of wholeness is without limitation. The degree to which we experience this directly correlates to how deeply we engage and embody it. Remember, we cannot shrink to greatness. Even when we forget, doubt, fear, or deny reality, words of praise and thanksgiving reactivate and restore us.

As we become more conscious of our perfection, we begin to heal the past and the future in the present. As we live more from the requisite faith in God as Source and from gratitude, we attune ourselves to the perfect pattern of wholeness.

— Published in the March 2013 Science of Mind *magazine*

# Give Thanks

*I rejoice in the bounty of God,*
*constantly manifesting as overflowing supply here and now.*

— Catherine Ponder

Let's expand into the full, overflowing, and infinite possibilities of our good this Thanksgiving. Let's do this not just in celebration of our national holiday—a time for gathering with family and friends—but as a clear spiritual intention.

There is no *reasonable limit* to the bounty of good God offers us or that we might accept. As Ernest Holmes writes, "Giving, I receive, and receiving, I give out again, thus increasing the divine bounty that meets me at every turn." What if, just as a drill during this season of thanksgiving, we truly embrace that divine bounty meets us as we approach it? What if we begin to trust, accept, and affirm, "My cup is filled and running over"?

Regardless of the degree to which we perceive our cups as half-filled or half-empty, or even if we claim we can no longer locate our cups, I issue the call for us to find our cups (look within) and lift them high in willingness, trust, expectancy, acceptance, and thanksgiving. This is an invitation for us to expand the capacity of our cups by living from the inside out—acting with spiritual discipline and from thanksgiving.

Life already provides all we need. It is time for us to develop greater mastery in releasing and letting go of struggle, strife, resistance, doubt, and fear. We must become more adept at blessing, receiving, and accepting. We must commit to being more loving, compassionate, inclusive, and expectant of good. This Thanksgiving, let's develop our spiritual discipline and transmute our horns of plenty into the horn of God's abundance. We will fill it to overflowing with love, peace, harmony, and blessings for all humanity.

Why stop there? From now on, let us make every day Thanksgiving Day—a day of praise and thanksgiving, a time to recognize and accept the bounty of the Divine and eternal goodness.

— *Published in the November 2013* Science of Mind *magazine*

# It's Already Done

*Healing is not creating a perfect idea or a perfect body; it is revealing an idea that is already perfect. ... Healing is not a process; it is a revelation.*

— Ernest Holmes

Infinite Mind surrounds us, responding to our thoughts according to law. Healing the body temple, transforming circumstances, and attracting good through the power of right thinking require deep, unshakable faith. Our work is to resist the temptation to doubt and, instead, accept the amazing power available to us through right thinking and perfect faith.

This practice is less about willing or trying to force an outcome than it is about accepting what is already given. It requires that we shift our thinking, expand our minds, and open ourselves to the infinite good already available. Deep, unshakable faith, once acquired, sets our sails, galvanizes our thoughts, and informs both the thinker and Universe that our intent is in alignment with perfect order—a formal invitation to bring it on.

It serves us to remember that our good awaits us when in our darkest moments, even when we, like the prodigal son, are at our lowest. In Scripture, the prodigal son, upon returning home, was immediately greeted by his father and reminded, "All that I have is thine." This is true for us, as well. All that the Father has is ours.

Accepting our good requires a healing in mind. The mission—should we choose to accept it—to heal our minds begins with aligning our thinking, vision, intentions, beliefs, actions, and acceptance with the bountiful good. However, we might first need to invoke a deep and perfect faith to neutralize past negative programming. As soon as we are less encumbered and distracted by thoughts of lack, limitation, doubt, and fear, we receive immediate access to the desired life experiences that our former thinking blocked.

As we heal our thinking and up-level our acceptance, we reveal that our heart's true desires already are provided. Indeed, all that the Father has is ours. And we had it all the time.

— *Published in the March 2014* Science of Mind *magazine*

# Pay Attention to Divine Frequency

In his book *For the Inward Journey*, Dr. Howard Thurman writes of the "glad surprise." He writes, "The *glad surprise* ... carries with it the element of elation, of life, of something over and beyond the surprise itself. ... The simple joy that comes when one discovers that the balance in the bank is larger than the personal record indicated—and there is no error in the accounting. The report from the doctor's examination that all is well, when one was sure that the physical picture was very serious indeed. All of these surprises are glad!"

Our lives are full of *glad surprises*. However, we frequently discount or overlook these surprises entirely. Some of us maintain a certain mindset that has us look almost exclusively through a prism that distorts and projects our personal universe through worst-case scenarios. Some of us feel as if we live in a game of chance, at the effect of the capricious whims of Lady Luck. Some of us become worn to exhaustion by recent and long-term disappointments, living through our pain and grief. And yet, there are glad surprises around all of us. The key is to pay attention and tune into the divine synchronicity in every experience.

A friend recently shared about his increasing anxiety regarding his dwindling bank balance and cashflow. Within a week, his update to me featured a glad surprise in the form of a letter from the state announcing unclaimed funds held, in his name, in a dormant PayPal account. He recalled that "something" told him to open this piece of mail. He also shared that due to his mounting pessimism, he almost discarded the envelope without opening it. When he and I focused on his key learning experiences in the situation, we revealed the following:

- Do not overlook your glad surprises.
- Stop the monkey mind and quit anticipating the worst outcomes.
- Look for evidence of good and embrace each blessing.
- Listen for and attune with Divine guidance.

— *Published in the April 2014* Science of Mind *magazine*

# This Far by Faith

*Doubt is a pain too lonely to know that faith is his twin brother.*

— Kahlil Gibran

In celebration of Black History Month, I lift up our ancestors of African ancestry. I invite you to join me in paying homage to those legally enslaved in these United States for hundreds of years, who later, once slavery was illegal, found themselves still forced to labor in economic and penal servitude.

Though enslaved, countless still were impelled by faith, human dignity, and a commitment to liberty to make a zealous demand for freedom.

Slave narratives reveal that many used their wit to devise creative schemes for escape, often aided by Quakers and other allies along the Underground Railroad. Even today, lawyers and advocates with various innocence projects commit themselves to legally freeing those wrongly imprisoned in our criminal justice system.

Dr. Martin Luther King Jr. understood faith. He said, "Faith is taking the first step, even when you don't see the whole staircase."

This seems a proper metaphor for those who could not and did not stay enslaved, who risked their lives for freedom. It also aligns with their White allies who risked their entitlement and safety and invested time, energy, and resources to secure freedom for their fellow humans—those enslaved in America's peculiar institution and immoral economic system.

Yes, all of this definitely took faith.

And what is faith? Ernest Holmes said, "Regardless of how exalted it [faith] may be, it is only a definite way of thinking. Broadly speaking, faith means a conviction about something that is stronger than anything that may appear to deny it."

Matthew 17:20 describes this faith: "Truly I tell you, if you have faith as small as a mustard seed, you can say to this mountain, 'Move from here to there,' and it will move. Nothing will be impossible for you." Faith is unwavering, unaffected by appearances or conditions, no matter where we are. Faith, even if this size of the mustard seed, is unmovable, non-doubting, and steadfast.

We find our unity in faith echoed in the familiar chorus sung at traditional churches and Civil Rights marches: "No turning around. We've come this far by faith."

We need a faith in the creative Intelligence in the universe, faith in the fact that things can be better, and faith in the spiritual causation back of all things so appearances do not confuse us.

*— Published in the February 2015* Science of Mind *magazine*

# The Joy of Answered Prayer

*The root of joy is gratefulness . . .*
*It is not joy that makes us grateful;*
*it is gratitude that makes us joyful.*

— Benedictine Brother David Steindl-Rast

My youngest nephew basks in the joy of being a freshman enrolled in the college he dreamed of attending. He shared with me how he set his intention in the sixth grade to attend the premier college for his musical emphasis, nurtured his vision of getting accepted, behaved in ways consistent with his intent, and regularly affirmed his desired outcome.

This was a labor of love and a joyous trek for him. In calling forth the realization of his soul's sincere desire, his hopes morphed into prayer. He chose and envisioned this outcome and now experiences the joy and the blessing of answered prayer.

True prayer is borne out of our soul's authentic desire. With an ecstatic spirit and in an attitude of gratitude, we declare our desired good to manifest, now. When we pray from gratitude, we are sure to "be of good cheer," as suggested in Matthew 14:27, "But Jesus immediately said to them: 'Take courage! It is I. Don't be afraid.'"

Our cheerfulness is borne out of our joy. Joy emanates from love, opening our hearts to ever-unfolding good and an abiding sense of oneness.

I am blessed to watch my nephew express wisdom beyond his years. I watched him work through adolescent angst, invoking prayer and applying spiritual principle to his challenges. I see his maturation, as Dr. David Hawkins charted in *Map of Consciousness*.

In his map, Hawkins calibrates joy at the top of the scale, in the domain of advanced spiritual students and healers. He says, "Joy arises from within each moment of existence, rather than from any other source. ... A capacity for enormous patience and the persistence of a positive attitude in the face of prolonged adversity is characteristic of this energy field ... capable of [inducing] a state of love and peace."

This is how my nephew walks through the world. I often am in awe of his bright light and indefatigable spirit, of the way he makes a positive difference everywhere he goes and in all of his endeavors.

How does he do it? He beams joy and gratitude. "The joy of the Lord is his strength."

*— Published in the September 2016* Science of Mind *magazine*

# Ancient Wisdom

*I am asking you to believe. ... I am asking you to hold fast to that faith written into our founding documents; that idea whispered by slaves and abolitionists; that spirit sung by immigrants and homesteaders and those who marched for justice; that creed reaffirmed by those who planted flags from foreign battlefields to the surface of the moon; a creed at the core of every American whose story is not yet written: Yes, we can.*

— U.S. President Barack Obama, 2017 farewell address

Indeed, we can. Many of us, especially those of us raised before the 1960s and those marginalized and oppressed by dominant-class policies, could not focus on appearances to discern our sense of self, personal power, and rightful place in the grand order of life. Instead, we invoked the ancient wisdom of the ancestors. Those who managed to survive the Middle Passage stood value added in the slave market and worked from "can't see to can't see," as opposed to from "sea to shining sea," building a country that largely denied their humanity.

Redlined and segregated to ill-equipped schools, health-threatening hospital facilities, and substandard housing (even now), we live in faith, continuing to embrace a vision beyond appearances and our current circumstances. We manage, as Dr. Howard Thurman wrote, "to keep fresh before us, our moments of high resolve." We know, regardless of appearances or policies, we, too, have an inalienable right to life and to live fully in freedom to pursue our highest good—a world that works for everyone. In faith, we believe.

Ernest Holmes's personal declaration of principles, later published as Centers for Spiritual Living's "What We Believe" statement says, "We believe in the individualization of the Spirit in us, and that all people are individualizations of the One Spirit. ... We believe in our own soul, our own spirit, and our own destiny, for we understand that the life of all is God."

When Holmes wrote these principles in 1927, his declaration may have seemed to be a new thought. Today, we recognize it as the ancient wisdom our ancestors practiced to maintain their sanity by recognizing and honoring their own divinity and acknowledging the same in all humanity.

This is fundamental to how we ultimately call forth a world that works for everyone. We must first accept this as our responsibility to demonstrate. We must believe we can. And then we will manifest this.

*— Published in the April 2017* Science of Mind *magazine*

# Eye on the Prize

*The Spirit of the Lord God [is] upon me; because the Lord hath anointed me to preach good tidings unto the meek; he hath sent me to bind up the brokenhearted, to proclaim liberty to the captives and the opening of the prison to [them who are] bound.*

— Isaiah 61:1 (King James Version)

I recently realized that all of my heroes' and sheroes' contributions to the planet breathe new life into Isaiah 61:1 and offer confirmation that each of us has a calling on our life. Each one of us is anointed. I interpret this scripture as a coded message about our individual and collective responsibility for executing what is ours to be and do. There is a calling for each and every life to serve humanity and the universe. We are called to find our authentic voice and apply it in service to our life purpose. We are here to make a difference in each and every moment.

Bryan Stevenson is one of my heroes. He started the Equal Justice Initiative in Montgomery, Alabama, and dedicates his life to fixing what he thinks is broken about our criminal justice system.

Stevenson says he "learned that proximity to people who are suffering, who are in need, who are condemned, who are excluded, who are marginalized can be transformative. And even if you don't feel fully prepared for it, it has a way of energizing you. And I wanted to be the kind of lawyer who could make a difference in the lives of people who were very vulnerable."

Stevenson believes our character will not be judged by how we treat the wealthy and powerful, but by how we treat the poor and marginalized.

During a difficult trial, an older Black man, working as a janitor at the courthouse, voiced how proud he was of Stevenson as an attorney. He told him, "Keep your eyes on the prize and hold on."

I encourage those of us who believe we are connected to each other and are open to a future of compassion and justice for all of humanity to also keep our eyes on the prize. Hold on.

— *Published in the September 2017* Science of Mind *magazine*

## Secure in God

*The eternal God is my refuge, and underneath are the everlasting arms.*

— Deuteronomy 33:27

We sang these lyrics with fervor in most of the churches I attended in my youth: "What have I to dread? What have I to fear, leaning on the everlasting arms? I have blessed peace with my Lord so near, leaning on the everlasting arms."

Ernest Holmes offers, "The everlasting arms suggest Divine protection, complete certainty, and the assurance that all is well with the soul. And how could it be otherwise, since the spirit of man is God?"

I accept this as a declaration of our oneness in God. I think it also acknowledges our connectedness—a certain security, union, and the impossibility of separation. It reminds me that we are secure in God now, always, and in all ways.

This is an essential message for such a time as this. Not only are we inundated and stressed by wars and rumors of war, often overwrought by the intense focus on separation, conflict, judgment, and blame. The truth is, in every moment, we are but a thought away from peace, harmony, and true joy. The degree to which we feel and can experience a sense of safety, confidence, and calm is a function of where we place our attention and direct our energy. It is the degree to which we are willing to trust and "lean on the everlasting arms."

Indeed, regardless of appearances and the current contagion of fear, I am safe and secure in the everlasting arms of God. We are all safe, by right of consciousness. It is up to each of us to acknowledge the Divine Presence and sense the peace within and surrounding all things. Truly, "What a blessedness, what a peace is mine, [when I am] leaning on the everlasting arms."

— *Published in the October 2017* Science of Mind *magazine*

# A Bubble of Our Choosing

I recently watched David Letterman's interview with former U.S. President Barack Obama. Obama shared information about an experiment using the Google search engine that serves to illustrate the degree to which we each live in a bubble.

According to Obama, three people (a liberal, a conservative, and a moderate) were asked to Google "Egypt." The liberal received information on Tahir Square. The conservative saw information on the Muslim Brotherhood. And the moderate was taken to vacation spots on the Nile.

Each searcher's previously expressed history, interests, and biases drew a different response during the search. I think this is what Ernest Holmes meant when he said, "Whatever pattern we provide, that will be our demonstration."

Social media algorithms used as metaphor for the law of magnetism illustrate that people who engage life with an intention toward compassion, inclusion, and the incumbent transformation within their own lives will be presented with opportunities and information supporting compassion and inclusion.

Much as fish are unaware of the water in which they dwell, so we similarly may live unaware of the degree to which our negative thoughts and feelings magnetically draw these experiences. We cannot see what we cannot see. Our inner algorithms, our current biases, reinforce our energetic focus and field. We essentially beckon universal support for what we don't want. This also ensures that we will not have access to a trillion other options.

Tristan Harris, former Google design ethicist, says, "If you can make it trend, you can make it true." This quote gives me chills because this notion—that whatever is trending gets accepted as truth—does not exist strictly online. It also manifests in our culture and in how we see ourselves and relate to each other. It is simultaneously inspiring because it reminds me that I am responsible for setting a new trend of thinking.

Whenever I engage spiritual law and entertain consistent visions of our highest good, I also set an empowering trend in motion toward a higher truth—a world that works for everyone.

What is trending in your life at this moment?

*— Published in the May 2018* Science of Mind *magazine*

# Playing Full-out in Faith

*And he said, "Just as you have believed, let it be done to you."*

— Matthew 9:29

As spiritual beings having a human experience, we receive the call to live faithfully to the truth of our being. And in faith, believing in our individual and collective divinity, we play the game of life full-out. Although this is simple, it is not easy to do. Playing full-out requires us to:

- Bring focused awareness to our heart's desire, while not yet manifested but fully forming in mind.
- Wholly believe our desires can become real and are now manifested.
- Dismiss doubt and fear, whose habitual devastation does not diminish our sense of worthiness.
- Engage faith as more definite and concrete than any doubt or fear.
- Stand in faith so irrepressible it cannot be shaken by a prognosis, delay, no-show, lay-off, rejection, or another's opinion.

Ernest Holmes reminds us, "Faith is a mental attitude that is so convinced of its own idea—that so completely accepts it—that any contradiction is unthinkable and impossible. The barriers between you and your greater good are not barriers in themselves. They are things of thought. It is because of this that all things are possible to faith."

Rather than focusing on seeming barriers, deny them. Deny they exist and deny them entry into your mind. Stand fast, knowing the Divine has no barriers. Recognize there is that within and around each of us always providing the ideal breakthrough. To stand in faith means we assume a position similar to Yeshua's when he declared, "Father, I know Thou hearest me always." We, too, must know we are guided by divine wisdom and that our thought has tremendous transformative power.

It has been said that Yeshua's key message can be synthesized to: "It is done unto you as you believe." This impartation of divine wisdom can be radically transformative, literally a game changer.

Something will always challenge your faith. Trust that there is something greater than your circumstances. The only question is whether you believe this. Remember, it is done unto you as you believe.

*— Published in the June 2018* Science of Mind *magazine*

# Tomorrowland

*In every moment, there's the possibility of a better future, but you people won't believe it. And because you won't believe it, you won't do what is necessary to make it a reality. So, you dwell on this terrible future. You resign yourselves to it for one reason—because that future does not ask anything of you today.*

— Governor Nix in the movie *Tomorrowland*

I have been smitten for a while by the theme, plot, and discourse in the movie *Tomorrowland*. This spring, I was at a music festival at the Palau de les Arts Reina Sofia in Valencia, Spain, and was astonished to recognize its architecture from key scenes in that movie.

This realization thrust me back to the optimism I felt during my first viewing of the film in 2015. I remembered how inspired I was by the simplicity of faith and power in "knowing how things work." I was further enthused by the clever reminder of the infinite possibilities available to anyone willing to "feed the right wolf."

When I returned from Spain, I immediately watched the movie again (for the fourth time). I feel Governor Nix's monologue is the perfect exhortation to hold our feet to the fire for such a time as this. There is indeed a consequence to believing and acquiescing to unfavorable or harsh outcomes. Whenever we subscribe to or invest our precious attention in what we *do not* want to experience, we are in effect "dwelling on this terrible future."

Nix's notion that rather than being willing to act, to be and do whatever is required, and to call forth an alternative outcome, we resign ourselves to the status quo and a terrible future.

Ernest Holmes offers, "As consciousness extends its vision, it extends the possibility of its objective experience. This means that objectively we possess that which subjectively we encompass. Our soul is always building a habitation for us because consciousness is forever dealing with first cause, with the causeless cause."

This is how we, in *Tomorrowland* terms, "feed the right wolf" and hearten our most desirable outcomes.

Our collective desire to demonstrate "a world that works for everyone" requires that we individually engage and apply a basic tenet of our teaching: Consciously or unconsciously, whatever we consistently dwell on (or feed) will ultimately manifest as our experience.

*— Published in the August 2018* Science of Mind *magazine*

# *I Didn't Falter*

*When the river was deep, I didn't falter. When the mountain was high, I still believed. When the valley was low, It didn't stop me. I knew...*

— Aretha Franklin and George Michael, "I Knew You Were Waiting for Me"

The morning I heard that the Queen of Soul, Aretha Franklin, passed, I had an introspective moment. A dear friend passed just the week before, and I felt my grief deepen and fear creep in. So, as is my practice, I engaged my go-to meditation, pulled out a prescriptive song, and played it at maximum volume on continuous repeat.

Aretha Franklin and George Michael serenaded me while I danced my heart open. As I boogied, I recalled the times, too numerous to count, when grief seemed as insurmountable as towering mountains or deep rivers and when I felt trapped in the dark valley of regret and fear. As I moved to the beat, I felt the doubt, regret, and fear fall away. I literally experienced the song lyrics and the reality that "I found my way out of the darkness, [and] I kept my faith."

Fear is a belief in a lie, as the acronym points out: FEAR, false evidence appearing real. Faith is kryptonite to fear. While faith feels relaxed and open, fear feels tight and closed.

Alan Watts wrote, "To have faith is to trust yourself to the water. When you swim, you don't grab hold of the water because if you do you will sink and drown. Instead, you relax and float." As I danced and sang backup for the duo, I simultaneously relaxed and floated free. In faith, as we connect with our true selves and open to our greater self-expression, fear dissolves, and we experience the creativity of Spirit expressing through us naturally, consistently, and with ease.

The lyrics express my sentiments exactly: "I don't regret a single moment; when I think of all those disappointments, I just laugh." So, I followed instructions. I laughed. I discovered that laughing in the wave of grief, regret, or fear is both empowering and freeing.

We live in an unlimited universe. Once we untether ourselves from grief, regret, and fear, we are free.

— *Published in the November 2018* Science of Mind *magazine*

# Know Exactly Who You Are

Some time ago, early in my study of Science of Mind, I heard the story of the Golden Buddha statue in Thailand. Monks intentionally covered the statue in clay for hundreds of years to protect it from invading troops. When the monks attending to the treasured clay Buddha tried to move the statue, some of the clay cracked, and then it began to rain.

The monks placed a tarp over the clay statue to protect it. During the night, one of the monks took a flashlight and went to check on the statue. While examining the cracks, he noticed something shining. Curious, he began to chip the clay away, ultimately uncovering the solid gold Buddha hidden beneath for hundreds of years.

I see this story as a perfect metaphor for such a time as this. The appearance is that we are feeling the effects of partisan politics and living in the alphabet soup of ever-increasing "-isms." It is as if we have relegated ourselves to living our lives enclosed in the restrictive clay concealing our divine essence—the truth of our being. It appears many of us have forgotten who (and whose) we are.

Rev. Dr. William Barber, known for his prophetic voice and "Moral Monday" activism, reminds and unites us with who we truly are. He connects words and actions to build what he calls "restorative hope," gathering support for those courageous enough to speak up for human rights and attend to the "tragic realities of the poor and forgotten."

He calls us to faith. He calls us to chip away at our sense of separation and disconnection from each other.

Let us take to heart this reminder from Barber in the days ahead: "From Moses to Jesus, the Bible tells us that those who fought for justice—those who spoke truth to power, those who refused to accept that injustice and inequality had to exist and that there was no better way—always found themselves hated, hounded, and heaped upon with false accusations simply because they believed in the necessity of speaking and working for the cause of righteousness and building a more just community.

"This lack of majority support is why the just must live by faith and must know exactly who we are."

— Published in the November 2019 Science of Mind magazine

# Freedom Treks

I have always been in awe of Harriet Tubman's numerous treks to freedom. I have seen paintings depicting her carrying a lantern, as if it lit her path to freedom. If she carried a lantern, at some point, she would extinguish the flame, be enveloped in darkness, and be guided externally by the moon and stars and internally by divine light.

I sense that Mother Harriet knew to check in, engage her inner compass, and follow divine guidance. There is no question she was divinely guided in what to do, when to do it, and how to do it. She surrendered, and divine light illumined her way and guided her through the darkness. Though there were shadows along the way, they could not overpower divine light.

She trusted. She knew that despite the cover of darkness, there was always light within.

This is what God is. God is love and God is light. Her legacy reminds us that we are always surrounded and enfolded in God's divine light.

The lyrics of the song "I Knew You Were Waiting (for Me)" remind me of this truth and Mother Harriet's legacy of faith and perseverance. The lyrics read:

> *Like a warrior that fights and wins the battle, I know the taste of victory.*
>
> *Though I went through some nights consumed by the shadows, I was crippled emotionally. ...*
>
> *Somehow, I made it through the heartache. I escaped.*
>
> *I found my way out of the darkness. I kept my faith.*

Yes! This song is in steady rotation on my "Freedom" playlist, and I suggest we memorize the chorus and sing it out loud with Aretha Franklin and George Michael:

> *When the river was deep, I didn't falter.*
>
> *When the mountain was high, I still believed.*
>
> *When the valley was low, it didn't stop me.*

This unapologetic sense of our innate power and clear awareness of who and whose we are banishes darkness to the nothingness from which it came and reveals the light within the shadows.

Mother Harriet claimed her freedom by following her inner guidance and surrendering to divine guidance. Divine light illumined a "way out of no way"—through rivers deep, mountains high, and valleys low. This is our legacy as well.

— *Published in the May 2023* Science of Mind *magazine*

# It's Up to Me

Ever since I first heard Rev. Dr. Terry Cole-Whittaker speak and powerfully affirm truth, I was smitten. She was my formal introduction to Science of Mind. It was in the mid-1980s, and I was going through a difficult time, feeling broken and defeated. Rev. Terry spoke truth deeply into my heart and mind, and she buoyed my spirit. She made the truth plain. I remember reading the affirmations she sent me, declaring them aloud, and learning to write my own. This teaching saved my life, and my circumstances shifted rapidly. Up until then, I had not made a connection between my life circumstances and my thoughts, beliefs, and words.

I have heard it said, "When the student is ready, the teacher appears." As a new student of the Science of Mind philosophy, I learned and began to see that how I think determines what I do and how I do it, how I show up.

This insight helped me glean how it truly is "done unto me as I believe." Prior to this course of study, I had not understood how my word transforms my circumstances and everything in and about my life. Through this teaching, I realized I have innate power and had been misusing it. It was up to me to set a clear intention and use my power and my word for good.

Even though I learned this truth long ago, forty years later, I still catch myself thinking, believing, and behaving as if external influences—what others say and do—limit my good and determine my outcomes.

I am a work in progress. I continue to study, practice, and endeavor to apply this powerful truth in every situation and circumstance. I do my best to focus positive attention on my belief and vision, and to remember that this is how life gets to be the way it is.

To paraphrase Michael Jackson, I'm starting with the one in the mirror. I'm asking her to change her ways. No message could have been any clearer: If I want to make the world a better place, I must take a good look at myself and make a change in what I believe and how I live.

Yes, if it is to be, it is up to me.

— *Published in the July 2023* Science of Mind *magazine*

SECTION 3

# Oneness

## FROM THE INSIDE OUT

*Togetherness as one is real. It is perhaps the only thing that is real. I am referring to oneness. This is our essential state of being. Not only humans but all animals, plants, and things at the conscious level of being.*

— Steve Leasock

## We Are the Ones

"We are the ones we have been waiting for." Originally penned by social activist June M. Jordan as the last line of her "Poem for South African Women," the line famously appeared as the title for Alice Walker's book of essays, in a song by Sweet Honey in the Rock, and as a kind of campaign slogan repeated by U.S. President Barack Obama in 2008.

These compelling words remind us that each of us is responsible for the fate we create, that we are empowered to transform our lives. We also bear responsibility for our collective successes and failures. Ernest Holmes wrote, "We are one even while we are many, and since each of us is a part of the Whole, if we seek to destroy each other, we only ultimately hurt ourselves. This is the great lesson of life." We teach that we are all incarnations of the One Spirit, and that God can become *to* the individual only what God can become *through* the individual. Universal Spirit demonstrates through each person's ability to be, think, and behave.

In a sense, we are a community of social-spiritual activists, standing for and in service of love and the highest and best for all concerned. We accept that we are the ones—the ones called to declare, teach, and practice in truth. We are the catalysts for what we declare in CSL's Declaration of Principles: "The healing of the sick and the control of conditions through the power of this Mind." Our spheres of influence begin deep within and extend further than we might imagine into the world.

In my own center's—Heart and Soul's—vision statement, we say, "Through our intention to be love and spread joy, we engender reflections of the same and more in others." God in us blesses and expresses as a healing presence to everyone with whom we make contact.

As CSL's Declaration says, as Religious Scientists, "We believe in our own soul, our own spirit, and our own destiny; for we understand that the life of man is God." We are one in God.

—*Published in the May 2012* Science of Mind *magazine*

# Just Us

*The starting point is at the center of our own being. When we awaken to the Divine within us, It will reach out and embrace everything around us, and It will discover the same presence in people and in events and in all nature, for God is not separate from what He is doing.*

— Ernest Holmes

Sometimes, we find it all too easy to critique another's spiritual expression. On a day that we'd be better off putting the focus on ourselves, we may find ourselves observing others with intense judgment and then arrogantly pronouncing how they've missed the mark (the definition of sin). Maybe he told a lie or did not share enough. Perhaps she prayed too loudly, and they sang too off key. In truth, no one could ever meet a standard of spirituality that some of us set for others. And is it really they who fall short of our expectations?

This kind of judgment is like the slippery slope described in Matthew 7:3, where someone magnifies the speck in a brother's eye and ignores entirely the beam in their own. The awkward moment when we realize that "we have seen the enemy, and it is us" is a blessing. It is our cue to check ourselves, to acknowledge that we missed the mark ourselves in judging what looks so suspiciously like someone else's gross error. It is also an invitation to look within, where we can release whatever is obscures our intention to be more inclusive, compassionate, and forgiving—of ourselves and others.

In his keynote address at CSL's 2012 Convention, our newly elected Community Spiritual Leader, Rev. Dr. Kenn Gordon, asked us to be more understanding and accepting: "It is not one that is right and one that is wrong—it is *one*," he reminded us, adding, "It is a time for transformation. ... Now is the time to let go of all of our opinions and all of our judgments." This is our igniting spark for change.

Now is the time to unlock the potential that lies before us and open to an idea much bigger than the one we currently hold. Now is the time to be the change we want to see.

—*Published in the August 2012* Science of Mind *magazine*

# Break through to Boldness

*Mother-Father-God, there's a healing going on.*

— Jami Lula

One of my brother ministers shared his recent breakthrough to boldness. In anticipation of his client's arrival, he opened his front door and inadvertently left the security door unlocked. He was in the kitchen and distinctly heard Spirit say, "Go out front!" When he did, he saw a woman exiting his front door and realized his laptop was not where he left it. He called for her to stop, but she kept walking. He hollered, "Stop! You cannot have that!" She stopped and turned around, revealing his laptop and cord clutched to her chest.

"You cannot have that. Give it back to me now!" She offered it to him, and tears started to roll down her face. As he took the laptop from her, he asked, "Is there anything in your bag that belongs to me?" She said no, and opened the bag so he could see the contents.

That small act of being willing to show him the contents of the bag inspired him to repeat what Spirit was whispering in his ear. "Tell her you trust her." Trust her? He told her, "I trust you." Her eyes got big, and tears streamed down her face. "I trust you when you say there isn't anything more of mine in your bag. I know that you did what you thought you had to do. But I want you to learn from this. I want you to know you can make another choice." "Thank you," she said, as she fell against his chest and wept.

A bold shift from a sense of separation to an experience of oneness is required of each of us. If we are to have a better life, we must be consistent, definite, and conscientious in directing our thoughts and deeds toward our desired outcomes.

As Holmes wrote, "We think. Our thought is creative and as a result, our life is what we make it ... thought by thought." We must uncover, neutralize, and replace false thinking and let the perfect truth manifest as the renewed body of our affairs.

— *Published in the December 2012* Science of Mind *magazine*

# Imagine Me

Recently, while perusing the Global Awesomeness Report page on Facebook, I saw this quote: "Don't forget to fall in love with yourself first." It was attributed to the fictional Carrie Bradshaw of *Sex in the City* fame. Although tickled by the source, I began to imagine myself *falling in love with me first*.

I realized I very much wanted to experience falling deeply in love with me. I focused, often and consistently, on what I *really* love about me. I embraced me. I lifted up my proficiencies and positive attributes, and I began to feel a greater sense of self-compassion and self-acceptance. I also noticed my heart ever softening toward others. There were even a few individuals in my imagination who requested, and were granted, leniency and emotional asylum.

The love and acceptance I poured on me blessed others as well. I imagined that I heard John Lennon singing:

> *You may say I'm a dreamer,*
> *But I'm not the only one.*
> *I hope someday you'll join us,*
> *And the world will be as one. ...*
> *Imagine all the people,*
> *Living life in peace.*

Pick up any newspaper or turn on the news, and you'll find that war, natural disasters, violent crimes, and accusations of corruption command the headlines. While we may not be able to control the headlines, we do have full control over what we give our personal *airtime* to. Our imaginations have tremendous power and enormous bandwidth, always broadcasting on the inner screens of our minds. We can begin where we are now—with ourselves. Let's start to imagine ourselves more in alignment with how we want our world to be.

Lennon's invitation to join his universal dream of oneness could be turbocharged by Kirk Franklin's "Imagine Me" to further inspire us:

> *Imagine me*
> *Loving what I see when the mirror looks at me 'cause I*
> *I imagine me*

*In a place of no insecurities
And I'm finally happy 'cause
I imagine me.
Imagine you loving you, first.*

—*Published in the September 2013* Science of Mind *magazine*

## View from Afar

In 2004, I had an amazing opportunity to serve as a group leader at the Institute of Noetic Science's conference in Bali. I distinctly remember astronaut Edgar Mitchell sharing an epiphany he had in 1971 during his Apollo 14 journey to the moon—his personal journey to oneness.

On his return from more than nine hours on the Fra Mauro Highlands region of the lunar surface, he gazed out a window and witnessed a spectacular sight.

He said then and in interviews afterward, "The biggest joy was on the way home, in my cockpit window every two minutes, the Earth, the moon, the sun, and the whole 360-degree panorama of the heavens. ... And that was the powerful, overwhelming experience.

"Suddenly, I realized that the molecules of my body and the molecules of the spacecraft and the molecules in the body of my partners were prototyped and manufactured in some ancient generation of stars. And that was an overwhelming sense of oneness, of connectedness. It wasn't them and us, it was, 'That's me. That's all of it. It's one thing.' And it was accompanied by an ecstasy, a sense of, 'Oh, my God! Wow! Yes!' An insight, an epiphany."

I was captivated and so moved by his experience that over the past decade, I frequently revisited my sense of his journey.

In my imagination, increasingly more of us awaken and begin to behave as if we know, trust, and willingly surrender to our innate oneness. Our lives bear evidence that we value our connection to all life and hold each other and our planet in love and reverence.

Even today, I envision us working together to ensure the viability and longevity of our planet. I see us invested in crafting solutions from which we intentionally create the conditions in which all humanity thrives.

Mitchell's experience transformed his life, his perspective, and mine, too. Other astronauts also reported similar perceptive and spiritual shifts. Their shared experience from afar may assist more of us in also realizing that all of life is interconnected and originates from the same source. We are one.

—*Published in the December 2016* Science of Mind *magazine*

# Willing to Forgive

*Forgive and you shall be forgiven.*

— Luke 6:37

This scripture is a clear declaration of freedom. It says to let go and, as you do, you are simultaneously set free. I know—it sounds too simple, too good to be true. I like to imagine forgiveness as an infomercial: "Forgiveness dissolves negative blocks, mental and emotional burdens from the past, *and* activates the healing power and presence of love."

Hype aside, the requisite order is clear: If we would be forgiven, we must first forgive. And as we forgive, we are forgiven.

The law of forgiveness is mental. It unveils and draws us closer to the whole, perfect, and complete core of our being. However, when we balk and refuse to let go—to forgive—we are, by law, simultaneously refusing to accept our ever-present good. Our resistance and grudges alienate us and interfere with the divine vibration and flow of good. What we refuse to give, we cannot accept.

We have no right to ask more of the law than we are willing to give of ourselves. Refusing to let go of judgment, condemnation, or retribution leaves us steeped in this negative vibration and perpetuates a negative cycle. None of us is immune to the residual charge or current triggers from negative experiences. Engaging forgiveness helps neutralize our triggers and corrects our perceptions of the past. Forgiveness offers us direct access to a positive shift in perspectives and invites the incumbent grace and ease into our new awareness.

During this time of fracture, fear, and divisiveness, I rely on the stories of healing miracles that abound in scripture and in common culture. In them, we release our mental, emotional, spiritual, and physical blockages. We heal through forgiveness.

When we release our resistance, rigid opinions, and negative perspectives of an experience or an individual, we open ourselves to experience a positive shift and we gain access, through our new perception, to a higher vibration. Holmes reminds us, "We cannot afford to hold personal animosities or enmities against the world or individual members of society. ... Love alone can beget love."

—*Published in the December 2018* Science of Mind *magazine*

# The Flow of Divine Choreography

In the mid-1970s, playwright Vinnette Carroll wrote and directed a soaring Broadway musical, "Your Arms Too Short to Box with God," based on the Easter Passion play and crucifixion as portrayed in the Book of Matthew. I saw it multiple times, mesmerized by the skillful acting, singing, and dancing. It was expertly choreographed and directed to convey a powerful metaphor. My current sense of this complex psycho-drama is that it meant to illuminate tragic, but empowering, human themes and unveil the ultimate dance of self-realization.

In truth, life is a dance, and we all engage in multiple simultaneous dances—the solo dance we do with ourselves, dances we choreograph in relationships, and the dance we do with the Divine.

Dancing, by definition, is "the art of moving in accord, often with a set pattern or choreography." I aspire for my dance with the Divine to be in the flow, engaged in meaningful connection and intimacy with the Divine in all life. When I have this experience, I am imbued with a sense of freedom, love, and oneness.

Regardless of our worldly dance moves—twirling, jumping, sliding, and any other foot and body movements—the Divine remains consistent and constant in Its loving presence and accepting nature. It is the origin and source of the very energy with which we move, breathe, and have our being.

The lyrics of one of the songs in the musical serve to remind that each of us is expected to dance our unique dance:

> *Everybody has his own way, my Lord.*
> *You've got yours, and I've got mine.*
> *Everybody has his own way.*
> *I go to church on Sunday morning...and [you] go Saturday at noon.*
> *It makes no difference when you go,*
> *as long as we feel Him in our room.*

The eternal continuum of life reveals a divine choreography, supporting and expanding our conscious awareness of our divine connection with the One. Your role and responsibility is to show up, go as deep as you possibly can, dance like your life depends on it, and express the divinity you truly are.

—Published in the April 2018 *Science of Mind* magazine

# Set Everyone Free

*I am not included within the pale of glorious anniversary! Your high independence only reveals the immeasurable distance between us. The blessings in which you, this day, rejoice are not enjoyed in common. The rich inheritance of justice, liberty, prosperity, and independence bequeathed by your fathers is shared by you, not by me. ...*
*This Fourth of July is yours, not mine. You may rejoice, I must mourn.*

— Frederick Douglass

These United States have, in many ways, changed dramatically since July 4, 1841, when Frederick Douglass spoke those words at an Independence Day celebration in Rochester, New York. And yet, a campaign persists to reject some based solely on their nationality, gender, ethnicity, sexual orientation, economic status, or other defining characteristic. U.S. history and culture benefit from the affirmations and actions of abolition-activists, too numerous to name or number, who remain committed to oneness, human rights, and restorative justice. The original abolitionists knew then and we must remember now what Fannie Lou Hamer said: "Nobody's free until everybody's free."

Indeed, ensuring others are perceived and treated as less than whole and restricted from enjoying basic freedoms guarantees that all of us are held bound in a continuing pattern of discrimination and exclusion.

If we are truly committed to our purpose to awaken humanity to its spiritual magnificence, then it is also ours to see and engage all people as whole, perfect, complete, and free.

As Religious Scientists, we begin in mind, affirming the humanity and rights of all and denying the inferiority, superiority, or seeming validity of any discriminatory strata.

We must be willing to see and actively include everyone in the divine fold. Otherwise, those whom we exclude are, as Holmes wrote, "like everyone else, 'an infant crying in the night'—something trying to be made whole, something with a deep yearning for security, a deep and unspeakable longing for love, for protection, and for peace."

This is ours to do. We can begin by engaging our imaginations to see, first in mind, everyone free, safe, and beneficially included—even before our mores and laws are reformed to honor all of us.

*—Published in the July 2018* Science of Mind *magazine*

## Centers of God's Consciousness

*Within this Infinite Mind each individual exists, not separated, but as a separate entity. We are a point in Universal Consciousness, which is God, and God is our Life, Spirit, Mind, and Intelligence. We are not separated from Life, neither is It separated from us; but we are separate entities in It, Individualized centers of God's consciousness.*

— Fenwicke Holmes

That we can all legitimately claim and highlight our different perspectives, experiences, and attributes is a given. However, acknowledging that at our core we are one is more complex. Unwisely, we focus predominantly on our differences—gender, ethnicity, sexual orientation, class, height, weight, etc.—and default into a mindset of duality.

Our shared culture is replete with duality frames and habitual patterns of separation that serve to undermine the elegant truth: We are one. These patterns of erroneous thinking also erode our innate power and personal responses. Absent an authentic sense of being "individualized center of God's consciousness," we tend to see ourselves as victims, at the effect of life, disconnected from a sense of our true self. We fail to see and honor our inherent divinity.

In this state, we are hard pressed to reason our way from victim consciousness to oneness. However, our lack of awareness does not alter the truth. In I Corinthians 12, we find this empowering metaphor: "Because the body is one and there are many members in it, while all of them are many members, they are one body." Even with all of our distinctions, we are still one body. The scripture continues, "For also the body is not one member, but many. For if a foot should say, 'Because I am not a hand, I am not of the body,' is it therefore not of the body?"

The truth is that each of us is an individualized center of God's consciousness, each an essential separate entity in It, each beneficial to the whole of humanity.

There is no benefit in comparing ourselves to others or questioning our innate value based on our differences. The foot and the hand are both of the body, just as you and I are of the Divine. In our uniqueness, we are one.

—*Published in the April 2019* Science of Mind *magazine*

# Namaste: God in Me Sees God in You

> We are one from the very start. We are one deep down in our heart.
> We are one, and that's the way it is. We are one.
>
> — Frankie Beverly and Maze, "We Are One"

Maze's song, "We Are One," is a major concert-crowd pleaser. The audience always sings the chorus of this 1983 hit song aloud, right along with the band, with unbridled passion and in a variety of keys: "We are one!"

You might expect our enthusiasm to also transform our forthcoming parking lot exit into a more enlightened experience. Not usually. After we breathed life into the lyrics and felt our hearts expand during the concert, why then do we not choose to recognize our oneness and honor it as we exit the parking lot?

We will continue to find it difficult to recognize ourselves in others while we hold them as "others." Sometimes it's super easy to recognize myself in another. In my family of origin, I am and have always been the spitting image of my father. Whenever anyone saw my father and me together, or even saw just a photo of him, the agreement was unanimous: When you see the daughter, you also see the father.

Over the past few decades, I have come to also recognize my mother's features morphing into the image in my mirror's reflection. It was also surprisingly easy for me, while in Tokyo, to see myself in several Japanese people on the city's streets and on the bullet train. We shared a spontaneous fascination with our similar features, high-contrast skin colors, and different hair textures. Indeed, it was a surreal and yet valid connection.

Holmes wrote, "Every act of human affection and love, of generous giving and receiving, of kindly relations with others, is an extension of the Spirit of life flowing through us—life, the great giver and each one of us, a distributor. This was the first great teaching of Jesus, that we should recognize this Divine Presence in everything and in everyone and in ourselves."

This is simple but not easy. We are called to recognize the Divine in all. The challenge is that this requires that we first recognize our own divinity. The key is to acknowledge the principle, embrace the power within, and live from our oneness in the Divine. We are truly one. The God in me recognizes the God in you. Namaste.

*—Published in the May 2019* Science of Mind *magazine*

# Carefully Taught

*You shall love your neighbor as yourself.*

— Matthew 22:39

Unfortunately, people loving, advocating for, and protecting the environment while ignoring our planet's most vulnerable human inhabitants happens every day. That said, I am particularly grateful to the heroes and sheroes who stand boldly for the rights, safety, and dignity of those who have been ignored, shut out, and restricted from access to the basic services and privileges most of us take for granted.

Fortunately, the list of activists and advocates, as well as our recognition of them, continues to expand. During this year's Gay Pride month, the online magazine *Qweerty* named Tony and Grammy award winner Billy Porter one of the Pride 50, honoring those "trailblazing individuals who actively ensure society remains moving toward equality, acceptance, and dignity for all queer people."

For me, Porter is a hero, one who stands in the gap as a steward for humanity while instigating the changes many dream about. Porter's duet with singer India Arie, a version of "You've Got to Be Carefully Taught," is included on his *Billy Porter Presents the Soul of Richard Rodgers* studio album.

The lyrics of this Rodgers and Hammerstein tune remind us:

> *You've got to be taught,*
> *before it's too late,*
> *before you are six or seven or eight,*
> *to hate all the people your relatives hate.*
> *You've got to be carefully taught.*

Working toward equality, acceptance, and dignity is essential because, unfortunately, too many of us have been carefully taught. Porter is actively engaged in creatively un-teaching us. His outrageous I-Am-ness offers a new paradigm of acceptance.

I am grateful *Qweerty* selected Porter. He is an extremely engaging, clear, and outspoken advocate with a decidedly unapologetic fearlessness. In the interview I saw, he is positive, hopeful, and empowering, always carefully teaching another way of perceiving our current circumstance and what is possible. He conveys a welcome raw clarity, saying, "We are on the precipice of a modern civil war, so it's time to stop taking a bag of popcorn to a gun fight. We have to stop in-fighting each other and band together to save our democracy and Earth's humanity. Period. The end."

*—Published in the September 2019* Science of Mind *magazine*

# Holy Encounter

*When you meet anyone, remember it is a holy encounter.*
*As you see him, you will see yourself. As you treat him,*
*you will treat yourself. As you think of him, you will think of yourself.*
*Never forget this, for in him you will find yourself or lose yourself.*

— A Course In Miracles (ACIM)

Holidays in general, and this holiday season in particular, seem to have their share of high expectations and increased stress. Seasonal engagements bring increased social connections, more public encounters, and challenging family gatherings. We put on our best drag and persona, making every effort to portray a holiday spirit of jubilance, ease, and accessibility. We join in the spirit of the season and attempt to forgive and forget, or at least let bygones be bygones, and give any unpleasantness between ourselves and others free passage.

We truly want to be cheerful, especially this season, so we strive to be the perfect demonstration of all that we believe the season should be. However, no matter how festive our attire or how cheerful our demeanor, we cannot make what is already holy any more perfect.

Author and spiritual teacher Ram Dass synthesizes the ACIM reminder above into a key practice we can engage for success during these holy days: "Treat everyone you meet like God in drag." As we set an intention to see everyone we meet as "God in drag," we simultaneously shift our viewpoint about the life we live and those we encounter along the way. We now accept our call to see beyond the surface or beyond our own biases and perceive ourselves and others more lovingly. Our objective is to sense and acknowledge that there are no others: There is only One. Acknowledging another is a holy encounter.

Let us begin this practice immediately while on public transport or driving, in the workplace or at home, and certainly during church or social gatherings. We are our best selves whenever we execute the holy practice of recognizing and honoring our oneness with everyone and everything. Stevie Wonder said it best: "You are me and I am you," and that *is* holy.

How joyful to recognize everything is holy *right now,* exactly as it is. Happy holy days.

—Published in the December 2019 Science of Mind *magazine*

# Calling All Good People

*I watched from my window as they gunned down unarmed men*
*Tried to say it's not my problem: couldn't happen to my friends*
*But the truth is they're my brothers, and they're my countrymen.*

— Delta Rae, "All Good People"

Viewing *Just Mercy*, the movie about civil rights attorney and founder of the Equal Justice Initiative Bryan Stevenson, gave me pause to ponder what is ours to be and do. The film is a biopic of Stevenson defending a man convicted of a crime he did not commit. The defendant is sentenced to death and awaiting execution on death row.

As viewers, we glimpse Stevenson's spiritual fortitude, the inmate's humanity, and the lawlessness of some peace officers who swore an oath to honor and protect.

This pervasive absence of justice in our judicial system ensures a caste system designed to benefit inequitable economic and social strategies. I was struck by the silence and dishonest testimony required to ensure the scales of justice are held in this tragically unbalanced position.

This is not just a cinematic scheme. Nor is it relegated to our past. We see this played out daily in numerous civil and political scenarios where the omission of truth (whether fact or Divine Truth) is key to orchestrating an ongoing miscarriage of justice.

At Heart and Soul Center of Light, our community began the new year declaring, "20/20 in 2020," that we might see our way forward with greater clarity and a deeper intention for what "a world that works for everyone" truly requires of us.

Matthew 25:40 reminds us, "I say to you, as much as you have done to one of these my brothers, you have done that to me."

What truth is required of each of us that we all can truly be free? What can you do to lift up our fellow human beings as our beloved sisters and brothers? What defense might you offer in the face of questionable charges?

We fortify our power when we pray and work together for freedom and justice.

—*Published in the April 2020* Science of Mind *magazine*

# All One

The notion of connectedness and oneness as found in Malachi 2:10—"Have we not all one Father? Hath not one God created us?"—was likely written circa 445 B.C. That means humanity has had literally eons to master inclusion and act out our divine connectedness.

The wise ones among us continually remind us of the higher calling in our lives and all of our relationships. In the 19th century, Ralph Waldo Emerson said, "There is one mind common to all individual men. Every man is an inlet to the same and to all of the same." So contrary to folklore, there are no strangers, no aliens. We have no enemies. We are to recognize all humans as members of our divine, eternal kinship.

Emerson, in an 1862 edition of *The Atlantic* magazine, illustrated inclusion in action when he spoke about the Emancipation Proclamation. Standing for destroying the lawless repulsion of slavery—the enemy of the human race—he said, "Then new affinities will act, the old repulsion will cease, and the cause of war being removed, nature and trade may be trusted to establish a lasting peace." Indeed, we know the truth and have everything required to reclaim our oneness and to master inclusion.

Recently I watched with pride, dismay, and ultimately horror our interactions with and treatment of our brethren during various phases of the Covid-19 shelter-in-place experience. Initially, I observed how helpful, patient, and considerate we were with each other while standing in those horrendously long lines and before social distancing delineations were marked. Then, about sixty days in, I heard numerous reports of altercations and saw videos of adult customers spitting on service personnel. We lost sight of our humanity.

In my mind, our current work is to remember to re-member, reclaim our humanity and innate awareness of oneness, and reject the false myth of separation.

Since God is everywhere, wherever we are, God is, the One Mind is. Whoever is willing can discern and honor the One Mind in everyone they encounter. We must remember and endeavor to live as one with Spirit as It is manifest in all people.

—Published in the August 2020 Science of Mind *magazine*

# The Gift of Compassion

*Compassion and caring are the ties that bind us together in mutual understanding and in the unified attempt to uncover the divinity in each other. Compassion is the most gentle of all human virtues, for it is the outpouring of the Divine givingness through all.*

— Ernest Holmes

Compassion is love to the hundredth power when expressed by people with hearts that truly care and who are unafraid to show it. The late Honorable Representative John Lewis mastered living as a compassionate conduit. He lived a fully orbed life, committed to working on behalf of those whom the local, regional, and national laws failed to serve and protect.

His life continues to serve as a powerful example of how to combine fearlessness with the most gentle of all human virtues. Lewis was not afraid to get into "good trouble." He said, "When you see something that is not right, not just, not fair, you have a moral obligation to say something. To do something … to go out and seek justice for all. You can do it. You *must* do it."

Lewis's compassionate spirit, commitment to humanity, and loving guidance galvanized multiple generations into taking action. He called us into being whoever we must be and doing whatever we must do to create positive change. He advocated that we, too, must be willing to get in good trouble, necessary trouble.

Lewis recognized the Divine in all. He consistently connected with people in integrity, sensitivity, and truth. He clearly committed himself to honoring the needs of others, often risking his life in the process. His legacy and compassion remind me of India.Arie's song, "The Gift of Acceptance." In my mind's ear, I can hear Lewis singing:

> *We all want the same things from life,*
> *We want peace, love, and prosperity.*
> *But can we give up our need to be right?*
> *Give the world a present.*
> *Give the gift of your acceptance.*

These lyrics never fail to touch me, and I ask myself: Can we—will we ever—give up our need to be right and instead offer each other the healing balm and compassionate gift of acceptance?

What say you? Can we? Will you?

*—Published in the November 2020* Science of Mind *magazine*

# Better Together

*Be better together: for the planet and the people.*

— excerpted from Tokyo's 2020 Sustainability Plan

There is so much I love about our Centers for Spiritual Living's Declaration of Principles and our vision statement. Our stated intent is principled and unambiguous. In considering this notion of going further together, I focused on the word *further*. This fostered inquiry of whether our intention in going further together is to go deeper—being better together—or to move forward in the direction we are heading. Our proclamation to create a world that works for all and declaration of oneness is clear.

Diversity and inclusion are opportunities and in our best interest. This is consistent with who we are and who we are called to be. They advise us, much as emergency instructions on airplanes, to remember to put our own oxygen masks on first, advice containing two parts. We are told to place our mask on first specifically so we can then be of compassionate assistance to our fellow travelers, regardless of their ethnicity, gender, or who they love. Too often we put our on masks and breathe deeply while watching our fellow travelers gasp for air.

Perhaps our primary focus is best placed on going deeper to discern how the world has come to be the way it is now. I marvel with great dismay at our collective history of perpetuating policies and practices that ensure outcomes far less than the highest and best for all concerned. We have wounds to heal, fears to release, truths to tell, oneness to realize, forgiveness to embrace and love to express. We cannot allow our aspirational declarations to morph into spiritual bypass and derail our progress.

Togetherness is essential. I believe we all fare better as a cohesive population committed to humanity—*all* humanity. As Holmes reminds us, our objective is oneness, not sameness.

Our work is to acknowledge and honor our differences and provide all with equal access to housing, employment, education, and public resources. We must go deeper and forward to be better together.

—*Published in the October 2021* Science of Mind *magazine*

# The North Star

*A smile or a tear has no nationality; joy and sorrow speak alike to all nations, and they, above all the confusion of tongues, proclaim the brotherhood of man.*

— Frederick Douglass

I have felt a connection with Frederick Douglass since I was a youngster researching his life in our encyclopedia set for a history class presentation. I marveled at Douglass's appearance and his way with words. I had not yet learned that what I was being taught about the history of Black folk, especially during slavery, was woefully inaccurate and purposely painted an incomplete picture.

Douglass said that although he had been forbidden to read, he offered poor White children bread to help him improve his reading comprehension. As a child with a speech impediment, I felt a kindred connection, as I required support to learn to speak clearly. The circumstances of Douglass's birth seemed to predestine him to a life of servitude and suffering. However, his inner guidance—to which he fully responded—led him elsewhere. His story, belief system, self-confidence, and locus of control mirrored the same themes my parents drilled into us in the 1950s, when there was still restricted access and presumed limits to our upward mobility.

Douglass's writings and speeches are brilliant, compelling, and inspiring. I continue to be moved by his ideas, clarity, and unvarnished honesty. As a Black man who escaped enslavement, he was, not unlike some today, always in some danger based largely on his race and gender. Only in recent years have I recognized the spiritual principles at the core of his theses and now see him as a skilled metaphysician. We know he was deliberately traumatized, abused, and regularly beaten, and yet he managed to look within his experience and know something more.

In the quote above from the 1800s, he declares oneness. He reminds us that all humans, as sentient beings, have feelings. Through empathy, we can recognize and honor each other's feelings. It is through our connectedness that we intentionally sense, acknowledge, and respond to all humanity with compassion, acceptance, and inclusion.

—*Published in the May 2022* Science of Mind *magazine*

# Our Roots: Rebooting Our Awareness

*As you enter your garden and observe the bamboo tree, the grapefruit and the many other variations of form, you see each is rooted in the one creative soil, and each is individualizing out of this creative soil that which is unique.*

— Ernest Holmes

"You have a DNA match to explore." In support of my intention to construct my family tree, this subject line greets me in my email inbox a few times a month. This is how I recently reconnected with a fellow ministerial student from twenty years ago who, it turns out, is a cousin on my father's side. This DNA update transformed our sense of connection and belonging. I marvel at the difference this sense of connection—a sense of oneness—has been for me.

One of my favorite television programs is *Finding Your Roots* on PBS. I always am enthralled by the revelation of kindred connections and how DNA reveals the most astonishing history for some.

I recently watched a segment featuring actor John Leguizamo, in which he discovered he had both Inca ancestors and Spanish ancestors who conquered the Inca. I witnessed Leguizamo reboot and embrace all in oneness. In graceful acceptance of the irony of his ancestral roots, he acknowledged that he is of the oppressor and the oppressed: He is connected to both.

In 1992, scientists unearthed a 4.4-million-year-old female skeleton, nicknamed Ardi, in Ethiopia. Her remains are 1.2 million years older than the skeleton of Lucy. Until then, Lucy was the earliest hominid skeleton ever found. From that viewpoint, scientists regarded Ardi as the point from which humans evolved. Ardi is our known point of human connection.

I wonder what it will take for us, as humans, to sense, acknowledge and honor our roots and connectedness across millennia. What is required for us to reboot, accept, and live out our divine connection with all humanity, all life?

Holmes reminds us, "No two people are alike, and yet all people are rooted in that which is identical." Our reboot is to live from this awareness.

—*Published in the January 2023* Science of Mind *magazine*

SECTION 4

# Begin

## FROM THE INSIDE OUT

*We are a spiritual people. I have faith that these hard times are awakening us to a new unity and a reaffirmation of purpose.*

—Susan L. Taylor

# In the Beginning

"From the Inside Out," the heading of my monthly column in *Guide for Spiritual Living: Science of Mind* magazine, is a *beginning*, a genesis for me. It is an opportunity for us to draw from within, to create, share, explore, challenge, and set ourselves free.

I began studying this teaching and philosophy with Rev. Terry Cole-Whittaker in 1983. I was deep in "a dark night of the soul." Depressed and in despair, awake in the wee hours of the morning, flipping through channels, I recognized and embraced the truth affirmed by Rev. Terry's television ministry. My thirsty spirit slurped up this truth. My mind paused from regurgitating the past, my heart opened to infinite possibility, and my soul exhaled. I sat up in bed, grabbed pen and paper, and devoured the affirmations Rev. Terry offered. I used them like a salve, reciting them over and over, as I learned to embody my good and begin my transformation.

What I learned then and embody still is that inside of me is everything—absolutely everything—required for the most amazing adventure: *life*. Through this teaching and practice, I know that life manifests from the invisible to the visible. What goes on inside my mind, my heart, and within my emotions ultimately manifests in the external—*from the inside out*. I have always had everything required to manifest my greatest yet to be. It already is. I already am.

Since 1983, I have had many beginnings. My most recent and most compelling manifested two years ago (in 2010), when I founded Heart and Soul Center of Light. I'm living my vision in this empowering ministry that began as a seed planted long ago, deep within my being, and has thrust me, heart first, into the infinite field of possibilities. I see now that my heart held a divine seed that, properly nurtured, yielded an exponential harvest.

I invite you to join me for an opportunity to connect with what's already happening within us, manifesting as our world, and empowering us to choose again so we demonstrate the world we envision. We'll travel a path to freedom together and call forth our good—*from the inside out*.

—Published in the January 2012 Science of Mind *magazine*

# Through the Fire

At Heart and Soul Ministry of Light, ours is a new ministry. The first celebration service was held *just* two years ago. I found my move into the role of founding minister both exhilarating and frightening. I often felt overwhelmed by the doubt and fear that threatened to thwart my growth and my expanded vision for my life.

What I went through is quite typical. Too often, when our good is spread before us, we doubt and immediately plan our retreat to the familiar past. We also fear that to actualize the best in us, engage our innate power, and claim the highest good, we may have to walk through fire. Instead of backsliding or succumbing, we can recognize this as an opportunity to "feel the fear and do it anyway."

Ernest Holmes said, "Divine Power is delivered to us only in such degree as we love and as we are constructive." Clearly, we have love *and* work to do. We can begin by releasing and letting go of the *stuff* we procrastinate about, the *stuff* that no longer serves us, and the *stuff* that adversely affects our current intention and commitment to life. This is our essential excavation and demolition work. It's ours to do. Let's do it!

During our 2011 Summer of Our Forgiveness program, I found inspiration to do my required work in one of our theme songs, "Through the Fire," by Chaka Khan. In our sessions, we sang out loud:

> *Through the fire*
> *Through whatever, come what may*
> *For a chance at loving you*
> *I'd take it all the way*
> *Right down to the wire*
> *Even through the fire.*

If we are to honor the intent to live fully—being more loving with everyone and in everything we do—we can no longer allow doubt and fear to hinder us. To go the full distance, we must stay inspired and constructive "right down to the wire, even through the fire."

Rumi said it most elegantly: "Love is a fire; I am wood." Please understand when I say, *"Burn baby, burn!"*

—Published in the February 2012 Science of Mind *magazine*

## Shift into the Flow

I've heard it said that while we cannot go back and start over, we can start today to create a new ending. In John 21:6, Jesus is said to have suggested to his disciples who were fishing and not catching any fish, "Throw your net on the right side of the boat and you will find some." Scripture records that when they did, they were unable to haul in the net because of the large number of fish caught in it. This scripture reminds me that something more is always available.

Each moment is a new beginning, an invitation to shift and change, opening us to everything that has been provided for the soul's journey. How will we approach this invitation? Will we perceive it as an opportunity? Where do we believe this invitation takes us? Are we standing in opposition to or cooperating with change? Are we coveting our habitual/generational "stinkin' thinkin'"?

Holmes reminds us, "The Infinite Mind is forever conceiving new ideas, and the Infinite Law is forever producing new forms." Each of us is responsible for making the required shifts in thought to get in the flow of the all-good in its infinite forms and offerings.

On January 1 this year, our community began reading Ernest Holmes's *365: Science of Mind*, wisdom for every day of the year. The message for January 16 includes an affirmation for change: "Love is guiding me into a real and deep cooperation with life." This affirmation encourages us to release the past, let go of fear, and shift into the flow. Often, the slight shifts we make invite the most meaningful change in our lives—forever.

Right where we are now there is joy, peace, harmony, and prosperity. However, we may not be able to experience it until we shift our consciousness and, thereby, shift our perspective.

When that happens, *everything* can change. When we "throw our nets on the right side," we ease into the flow with direct access to the very good we seek.

—Published in the June 2012 Science of Mind *magazine*

## Together ... At Last

His Holiness the Dalai Lama, in reflecting on world religions, concluded that compassion lies at the heart of all religions and said that it is the "right time for inter-religious harmony to replace conflict, hatred, and misunderstanding." It is also the call to kinship and opportunity for our Centers for Spiritual Living to actualize our full intention for integration.

We had a taste of our future during the opening ceremony of our 2012 convention in a powerful prayer duo: Eugene Holden, RScP, and Rev. Erin O'Donnell Stanlee. Their power-filled opening prayer treatments were different than what we might expect. However, rather than a clash of cultures, we were treated to a delectable buffet, featuring Rev. Stanlee's prayer as the essence of our favorite grandmother's apple pie and Holden's as the flavor of Big Mama's prize-winning sweet potato pie.

Their diverse prayers illuminated an opportunity for us to see and transcend the cultural shift our integration requires. For some, this opportunity may manifest as fear. Some fear that our integration might make us a melting pot, requiring all of us to sacrifice who and how we are. In truth, we are destined to be an international and intentional gumbo inspiring us to discern our oneness and obliging us to be accepting.

As Holmes wrote, "A new light is coming into the world. We are on the borderland of a new experience. ... Happy are we if we see these things that, from the foundation of the human race, have been longed for by all aspiring souls."

None of us can thrive in isolation. We are connected, and each is impacted by what happens to the other. We are all enriched by our diversity, doubly so when we value each other and our diverse contributions to the whole.

An era of compassion and inclusion has been illuminated for the greater good of all, and it is time for us to step into this future together as one—manifesting a world that works for *everyone*. Can't you just hear Etta James singing in the background, "At last... ."

—*Published in the November 2012* Science of Mind *magazine*

# Begin Now

"We'd only begin to start living our lives/If today were the last of all days." These powerful lyrics from the song "The Last Day," by John Eubank and Brenda Russell, offer us an uncomfortable glimpse of a common reality.

Why should we wait for the last of all days when we can engage in significant new beginnings in each moment of our lives? Letting go of blame and embracing forgiveness are central here. It's a way of repacking our luggage for the journey ahead, leaving out the stuff that often weighs us down. It also helps eliminate any blind spots that prevent us from seeing the lessons of the past, which otherwise might hinder us in living our greatest yet-to-be.

Beginning anew includes awakening to our ability to change, change, and change again. Yes, I know, we all want transformation. But do we really want to change?

Some of us can offer personal testimony as to exactly how pain keeps pushing until vision pulls. Too often, we find ourselves rewinding the same old movie, mesmerized by the past. Not only are we captivated by past pain and suffering, we think everyone else should be as well. Consequently, we fill our airwaves with enhanced tales of our history and how awful it was. Our New Year's resolutions are often inspired by dissatisfaction with weight, debt, earnings, relationships, and the fear that this new year will end with us in the same or worse circumstances than at the end of the previous one.

It's time for us to flip the switch and begin to narrow our focus on the possibilities available now. That's all: Begin from right *now*.

Holmes reminds us, "The past is behind, and whatever doubt it may have held is gone with it. The future is before, bright with prospects…. Let us live in the present, looking neither backward in horror nor forward with apprehension, but looking into the present with joy—'abiding in faith.'"

—Published in the January 2013 Science of Mind *magazine*

# *Vivir Bien*

Many of us were present for the 2012 winter solstice and sensed the imbalance and fear around the "end of the world" theories. I pray that we also were tuned in for the Divine Ideal at the center of the chaos around the Mayan calendar's auspicious date— December 21, 2012.

Evo Morales, Bolivia's first indigenous president, often speaks of *vivir bien*, meaning "living well." His definition is about pursuing the collective good in balance and harmony with the Earth. When he addressed the United Nations, he said this date signals a turn toward the collective good: "According to the Mayan calendar, the 21st of December is the end of the non-time and the beginning of time, ... the end of selfishness and the beginning of brotherhood. It is the end of individualism and the beginning of collectivism... . It is the end of hatred and the beginning of love, the end of lies and beginning of truth. It is the end of sadness and the beginning of happiness. It is the end of division and the beginning of unity."

This shift in perspective calls for us to remember the Divine at the center of all transformation. Holmes said, "The Divine Ideal is the perfect image held forever in the Mind of God. The perfect body, the spiritual body, is the fulfillment of the Divine Ideal and is the real man that all of us hope to manifest. This is the pattern by which we try to bring out perfection in our lives. In each one of us, there exists the Divine Image of ultimate perfection, for God indwells everything He creates."

To realize this Divine Ideal, we must fully accept and nurture this construct of "living well" to complete manifestation. We would be well-served, as scripture suggests, to "keep thine eye single" as an exercise in maintaining our focus and intent on this collective good, to the exclusion of all else. When we recognize that the "end of the world" is also a divine beginning, we can choose our optimum state immediately as God's idea of us—whole, perfect, and complete.

—*Published in the May 2013* Science of Mind *magazine*

# One with the Father

Martha and the Vandellas's 1964 vocal inquiry is just as relevant today as it was then, and it's a great question for Easter: "Callin' out around the world, are you ready for a brand-new beat?" This *beat*, the true rhythm and flow of life—as old as time itself and yet vibrant, constant, productive, and expansive—is ever calling forth a new awareness and experience through and as us.

Our challenge is that some of us have not yet unpacked our old baggage to create space for a new beat. As long as we are tethered to the past, we limit our access to the gifts available to us at the present.

Neville Goddard taught that Easter is the art of dying to yesterday so that we may live today. I further see Easter as an invitation for us to die daily to the past so that we may live more fully in the present as the Presence. Accepting the invitation requires us to surrender our sacred-cow belief systems and any limiting perceptions of our past and present. It seems that a lot of gunk must first be released to allow us to access and dwell in the awareness that "I and the Father *be* one" and that "I am one with all that is."

The truth is that we are already one with all that is. Even so, this notion of oneness seems to stump us. Our response is similar to the disciple's response to Yeshua: "Master, this is a hard teaching." And it is—our eyes, our perceptions of past experiences, our interactions with others, and our worldviews all conspire to confirm separation and otherness. That's our old beat.

Drawing from Deuteronomy 6, Goddard offers ancient wisdom as a new beat:

Hear, O Israel: the Lord our God is one Lord. Hear, O man made of the very substance of God: You and God are one and undivided! Man, the world, and all within it are conditioned states of the unconditioned One, God. You are this One; you are God conditioned as man. All that you believe God to be, you are; but you will never know this to be true until you stop claiming it of another and recognize this seeming other to be yourself.

—*Published in the April 2014* Science of Mind *magazine*

# Taking a Powerful Stand

Some of the best examples of standing in our power can be found in the archives of nonviolent civil disobedience, especially the strategic protests in the American South during the Jim Crow era, protests that defined the Civil Rights Movement.

The first time I saw *Selma*, the film starring David Oyelowo as Dr. Martin Luther King Jr., I was particularly struck by the portrayal of harmony, diversity, and the sheer number of protesters who responded to Dr. King's call. They traveled from other states and countries to support the Voting Rights Protest and the March from Selma to Montgomery.

The film illustrates how one person standing in their power can awaken something in all of us. When we witness another in confidence and courage—standing for what is right and ultimately the highest and best for all concerned—it is as if we are into a magnetic field, drawn to stand in our power to make a difference as well.

Many of us joined churches and community organizations, supported and contributed to ambitious causes, often motivated by the stand the leader took and the power she conveyed.

Viewing *Selma* for the second time, I wondered whether we (or I, personally) are yet standing in our authentic power, intention, and actions to call forth a world that works for everyone.

I am motivated by what Frederick Douglass—the man who escaped slavery and soon after was recognized and respected as an orator, editor, and public servant—wrote in an 1846 letter to William Lloyd Garrison: "I am not only an American slave but a man, and, as such, am bound to use my powers for the welfare of the whole human brotherhood."

Douglass definitely stood in his power—power the law of the land said he did not have—and made a quantifiable difference in the abolition of slavery. When we stand in our power, we simultaneously use our powers for the good of all, just as he and others have done, to positively transform lives.

This is ours to do and we can do this. Remember, one and God make a majority.

—Published in the June 2015 Science of Mind *magazine*

## Awakened, Arisen, and Free

*Awake and arise from your sleep, and hear the words of our letter.
Remember that you are a child of kings, consider the slavery you are serving.*

— from "The Hymn of the Pearl," in a passage on the apocryphal acts of Thomas

Summer before last, our spiritual center offered a dramatic performance of "The Hymn of the Pearl." Ours revealed an urban hero's journey.

The hero's journey is our required rite of passage at a given stage of our lives. Our hero, initially portrayed as lacking in awareness and spiritual maturity, transformed himself as we watched and self-identified as he evolved to discover a greater possibility within himself, that he then began living.

Joseph Campbell coined the term "hero's journey" and identified several basic stages. These stages form the hero's progressive path for spiritual evolution. On this path, there is always a point of awakening that advances the hero's transformation into their greatest-yet-to-be.

Although our unique heroes' journeys are not synchronized with our annual calendar, we can surely begin 2016 in a conscious intent to become awake and arise.

In much the same way as my favorite biblical depiction of a hero's journey unfolds for the prodigal son, our journey also includes a point of spiritual awakening, the moment each of us comes to our divine self.

This awakening always occurs away from the hero's "home"—the former way of being. Though heroes may actually make a physical move, our journey is not negotiated in miles.

Our journey is a movement in consciousness. It is as if our hero, in traversing from past awareness toward a greater knowing, is living Isaiah 65:17 and wisely declaring, "For, behold, I create new heavens and a new Earth; and the former things shall not be remembered nor come into mind."

As we accept the gift of this new year, we also can choose to depart the mundane and seek the Divine. This is the perfect time to launch your next hero's journey.

Happy New Year! Happy New You!

*—Published in the January 2016* Science of Mind *magazine*

# Our Bright Light

*A good name is better than great riches, and loving favor than silver and gold. ... Train up a child in the way he should go; and when he is old, he will not depart from it.*

— Proverbs 22:1 and 6

As this winter season ebbed, so did the Earth-life expression of one of our wise princes. He departed this plane one month before his twenty-second birthday. The University of Southern California, where he was a student, and our greater Oakland community mourned his passing, as we embraced his parents and marveled at their grace and fortitude. Their son lived as an empowered mentor, change agent, master drummer, compassionate soul, and authentic, loving being. This young man, who was raised to be a son to his hometown of Oakland, was nurtured by our community at large. His living bore evidence of the truth of Proverbs 22:6.

Kahlil Gibran reminds us, "Your children are not your children. They are the sons and daughters of life's longing for itself."

We witnessed the overwhelming evidence that this young man was grounded in this awareness. He accepted and expressed his sonship in service to the community. He supported, served, and nurtured other young performers and was an outspoken advocate for Black Lives Matter, women, and gun control.

Some recognized his generosity, maturity, clarifying insight, and penchant for spontaneously teaching universal truth and fancied him a formidable future justice activist or statesman. He touched so many in his brief, impactful life.

None of us knows how long we have on this plane. Each of us must engage our faith in the future and claim our power in the present to live boldly and intentionally, always endeavoring to embrace an ever-increasing empowered consciousness.

Doing so would serve not just to honor his memory and that of the many other bright lights who are no longer with us, it would serve to ignite our spirit into being our highest and best and supporting others in expressing their best. Let us set our intention to shine our light brightly, as a torch passed across generations, toward those seeking to make a difference. May the torch we pass ultimately illuminate a world that truly works for everyone.

—*Published in the June 2019* Science of Mind *magazine*

# Kintsugi 2020

In these final weeks of 2020, I acknowledge this year as a time of tremendous change: Covid-19, virtual everything, natural disasters, international protests, 2020 U.S. elections, and civil discord. Then on a personal note—in the midst of all of this—our spiritual community moved into a new space. This was a year of full-on change.

Most if not all of us also have moved in, around, and through feelings of doubt, fear, joy, heartbreak, and exhilaration. Some of us sheltered in place or even quarantined, while others were either required to or chose to continue some of their previously established activities. We all simultaneously experienced death, loved ones passing from this realm to another or the end of something. And we witnessed birth during this time, whether in the form of new life or transformed relationships and experiences.

We have known both extreme strife and deep peace. We witnessed allies forming cohorts and getting into "good trouble," and we also lovingly released those whose silence and apathy hurt and perplexed us. We realized that our former normal was not a universal reality but merely race consciousness.

Before we commit to a new normal, we might apply what Kysha Mitchell suggests: "It is time to feel, find, and thrive." She advocates making space to feel our losses, emotions, and memories, and then find inspiration from our experiences and within our most challenging situations. She encourages us to use it all as fuel to thrive. She says, "In essence, break down the age-old paradigms in our minds of when we deserve to experience passion, purpose, and joy."

Drawing from Mitchell's wisdom, I include the Japanese art of *Kintsugi* in my acknowledgment and celebration of 2020. Kintsugi literally means "to join with gold." In Zen aesthetics, the broken pieces of an accidentally smashed pot should be carefully picked up, reassembled, and glued together with lacquer inflected with a luxuriant gold powder. There should be no attempt to disguise the damage. The point is to render the fault lines beautiful and strong.

So in deep gratitude, I bring all the brokenness of 2020 into a new and reimagined celebration of truth, fused with golden love, lacquered in faith.

—Published in the December 2020 Science of Mind *magazine*

# New Year, New Me

*This Spirit is happy, whole, free, filled with joy, eternal in Its existence and can provide you with everlasting expansion.*

— Ernest Holmes

As I write another New Year's resolution, my heart overflows with gratitude for, well, everything. Every life experience offered its unique blessing. Some experiences resulted in manifested prayer; others appeared as my worst fears. All morphed into whatever was required to reveal a greater truth, crack open my heart, forgive myself, or accept what I had been resisting.

I am grateful, especially in this new year, to celebrate the divine wonder of life—my life. I did not always know I could or would be here—here in peace, a deep inner peace; here in self-acceptance; here in joy; here living as love-in-progress.

There was a time when I could not have imagined this day, these feelings, and this knowing. I could not have begun to fathom my current life or even being alive. I could not see through the pain to envision my present joy.

I was stuck—deeply stuck—in self-loathing and a sense that I had no right to love or to even exist. Ultimately, when it felt too difficult to go on, I attempted suicide. Twice. Both attempts were made before I was even twenty-one.

I have tremendous empathy for my young self, how she saw her world and held herself in a limiting consciousness. Her life felt threatening, complicated, and doomed. She knew nothing of the principles I now study, practice, and share.

I now know I AM, that who I am matters, and I know whose I am. I could not access this truth back then. I had to first see me through empathy, compassion, and love before I could fully comprehend, accept, and begin intentionally applying spiritual principle.

I invoke Holmes's words: "The Law knows us only as we first know ourselves. We make up Its mind because Its mind is subjective." I have direct access to the "limitless wonder of the universe," and thanks to this teaching, I know God is love, and I rest in this ever-expanding love. I give thanks for a new year, a new me.

—*Published in the January 2022* Science of Mind *magazine*

# When I Think of Home

*When I think of home, I think of a place where there is love overflowing.*

— "Home," from *The Wiz*

When the lead character in *The Wiz*, Dorothy, sings this song, she reminds me of my own yearning to belong. Many of us did not grow up in families where we experienced overflowing love. Many of us still lick our wounds or work to heal scars developed in our families of origin.

Home is not a physical locale; it is a feeling to which we all aspire. In both the movie and Broadway versions of *The Wiz*, Dorothy takes us on a hero's journey in which she comes to realize she had what she needed most all the time. She did not experience love, acceptance, or a sense of belonging at home in the ways she yearned for or thought she needed. Yet, she came to realize she received love, acceptance, and a sense of belonging in the way that matters most—an inner, abiding sense of home. Sometimes, like Dorothy, we, too, must imagine the loving, peaceful homes our hearts desire.

As the song continues in my head, it reminds me of the many Science of Mind students, who, in expanded awareness, now see beyond some of the mental and emotional blocks they previously held. They feel empowered to call for a do-over. They see the past through new eyes and feel it with a healing heart. Like Dorothy said, "I wish I was home. I wish I was back there with the things I've been knowing. Living here in this brand-new world might be a fantasy, but it's taught me to love. So … it's real to me."

Students of Science of Mind realize this journey home is an inside job, and the brand-new world is revealed. Embracing this teaching and consistently practicing principle changes how they see and experience everything.

*The Wiz* reminds us that we must look inside our hearts to find "a world full of love—like yours, like mine, like home." Dorothy satisfied her heart's yearning for oneness, love, and authentic connection on her journey. This transformed the home of her heart.

Let us affirm, as Dorothy might, "I am at home in Love, in the place I never left."

—*Published in the November 2022* Science of Mind *magazine*

SECTION 5

# *Shift*

## FROM THE INSIDE OUT

*Be hopeful. Be optimistic. Never lose that sense of hope.*

— John Lewis

# On Point

I let the scale in my doctor's office intimidate me. I was apprehensive about what would ultimately be revealed and the adeptness required to move the appropriate weight to its perfect point. I literally held my breath until the weighted arm was at counterpoise. What a powerful metaphor.

The scale was designed and engineered in perfect balance, and so are we. But, like the scales, from time to time we find ourselves out of alignment, shifting far from the balance point—the place of grace and good awaiting us. Restoring this delicate balance begins with training our mind to return to center. Maintaining the balance, however, requires the determination to let go of what's not serving us well and the commitment to move toward behaviors and practices that support balance.

Ernest Holmes wrote, "The trained mind is far more powerful than the untrained mind." His wisdom changed my life. Training the mind is the key. It's like training our beloved pets. We all want our pets to be happy and free, but no one wants an untrained, wayward dog, running here and there, chasing cars, humping legs, and snapping at people. We want our pets to heel when we say so.

The same process works when training your mind. When you catch your mind running wild through the pain and despair of the past, reel it in. Pull on your leash and lovingly guide yourself back to your center point. Just say, "Heel!" It's that simple, and what a blessing.

We choose at all times whether to be a servant to our past or the master of our future. We must retrain our minds and recalibrate our hearts. Perfect balance, being on point, is God's great gift for us. It's a gift that we can choose the mental attitude, emotional state, and spiritual practice we want to experience. No matter how off course we may have gotten, choosing rightly restores balance.

With the highest intention and commitment, let's move toward the perfect point on the continuum—in the flow and on point.

*—Published in the April 2012* Science of Mind *magazine*

# Now I See It

*We do not change all of the patterns of our thought in a moment. Rather, it takes place little by little, until gradually the old thought patterns become transformed into new ones by some inner alchemy of the mind, the operation of which we do not see but the manifestation of which we do experience.*

— Ernest Holmes

In John 5, we are introduced to a "certain man who had an infirmity for thirty and eight years and waited by the pool at Bethesda for an angel to trouble the water so that he could be healed. Then Jesus saw him and asked, 'Wilt thou be made whole?' And immediately the man was made whole, took up his bed, and walked."

Don't let this powerful allegory trigger your tendency to be enamored by "overnight success" and ignore the preceding time and focus required for most success. My sense is that thirty-eight years by the pool may have supported the required shift in consciousness. Remember, we do not always see the shift in mind, but we do experience the manifest change.

We all have demonstrated this many times using meditation, prayer, and affirmations to shift our lives. I illustrated this truism during one of our services by pouring clear liquid into a glass container of dark-blue liquid until it turned clear. We gleaned a moment—*the tipping point*—when there was a critical mass of clear liquid sufficient to immediately change the overall concentration and appearance of the liquid. It was a variation on "now you see it; now you don't."

Malcolm Gladwell, author of the national bestseller *The Tipping Point*, defines this as "the moment of critical mass, the threshold, the boiling point." He preaches to our choir when he says, "Tipping points are an affirmation of the potential for change and the power of intelligent action. Look at the world around you. It may seem like an immovable, implacable place. It is not. With the slightest push—in just the right place—it can be tipped."

Let's push until we see it.

—Published in the October 2012 Science of Mind *magazine*

## Ask, Seek, Knock

Holmes wrote, "We do not know how it is that an invisible energy causes the sap to flow up in a tree, or how it is that a chicken comes out of an egg. We may only watch the process. No biologist knows what life is; no psychologist knows what the mind is; no philosopher knows what reality is; and no theologian really knows what God is."

Too often, we expect our experts to provide *the* answer. Sometimes, we are met at the level of our expectations by a so-called expert who offers a prognosis so limiting that it reveals their own mind to be full-to-overflowing with facts, while unable to embrace the field of infinite possibility. It is up to us to inquire more deeply of Truth. Matthew 7:7 reminds us, "*Ask* and it will be given to you, *seek* and you will find, *knock* and it will be opened to you."

Innocence and wonder—essential elements of the beginner's mind—are fuel for the fire of heightened interest and curiosity about life. Deeper inquiry, seeking beyond the apparent trajectory expands our capacity to sense and resonate in truth. It pushes us beyond our current awareness and gives us certain access to the field of infinite possibility. Once we begin paying closer attention and cultivating spiritual inquiry, we ignite and expand our "I-don't-know" mind. It is this aspect of the mind that we must train until we become comfortable with uncertainty.

To manifest a decided change from a present condition, we must first know what we want. Here, certainty is required. We must also train the objective mind to focus definitively on what we desire and simultaneously remain fluid and trusting that it is already manifest.

An authentic, open-minded curiosity and inquisitiveness are the keys to transformation. Discernment and the courage to inquire deeply are the precursors to spiritual inquiry. Most of all, we must be willing to *knock*—to counter what we previously believed and approach new ideas and opportunities with a sense of exploration, adventure, and, of course, faith.

*—Published in the July 2013* Science of Mind *magazine*

## A Simple Choice

Many of the beliefs we continue to hold and defend are little more than habitual ways of thinking. At some point, they no longer serve us. Either we changed or the context in which they were first formed shifted. I don't know about you, but I now embrace an entirely different belief about myself and my relationship with God than I did before I experienced the guidance of Rev. Terry Cole-Whittaker in 1981—my start in New Thought.

A perfect example of this is a piece written by former U.S. President Jimmy Carter:

> *My decision to sever my ties with the Southern Baptist Convention, after six decades, was painful and difficult. It was, however, an unavoidable decision.... The belief that women must be subjugated to the wishes of men excuses slavery, violence, forced prostitution, genital mutilation, and national laws that omit rape as a crime. [It] costs many millions of girls and women control over their own bodies and lives, and continues to deny them fair access to education, health, employment, and influence within their own communities. The impact of these religious beliefs touches every aspect of our lives.*

He closes with, "It is time we had the courage to challenge these views." This is a great reminder that we wield power beyond our axiom, "Change your thinking, change your life." In fact, when we change our thinking and stand for equality and dignity for all, we change not only our own lives. We change systems.

Whether it is gun control, same-sex marriage, tax reform, and more, we recently witnessed others stand for what they once had been against and vice versa. Their stands may represent a simple choice, and yet it still may be difficult to stand publicly in the new choice and *speak humanity to power*. We have amazing power within. We must summon the courage to challenge our views and embrace our faith to stand firmly in the change.

—*Published in the August 2013* Science of Mind *magazine*

# Our Perfect T.O.O.L.

*There is only One Life. That Life is God's life.
That Life is perfect. That Life is my life now!*

— Ernest Holmes

During our first service of 2014, our Heart and Soul Choir chanted, "There's only One Life." The spirit of love, grace, gratitude, and awe was palpable, and I am still tingling and vibrating in this realization of perfect truth. I continue to bask in the crescendo of energy realized when our desire, intention, and focus begin to form in our imaginal mind.

The more I chanted, the more connected and certain I was of the Presence and Power that creates everything out of Itself. I truly sensed this as perfect, whole, and complete. I came away more convinced than ever that this is *the* truth and the heart and soul of what we teach and endeavor to practice and live.

As we come to trust and surrender to the awe-inspiring Presence and Power, we also recognize that our desires are fulfilled in perfect time and perfect form. A story Neville Goddard shared about some children using what they learned in his Sunday school illustrates this:

> *One day the little girl, who is the youngest of the three, was quite sick, a beastly cold. That night when her brothers said their prayers, these are the words they used: "Thank you, God, that sister is perfect tomorrow." They could not look at the little girl, sick as she was, and say, "Thank you, God, that sister is well now," but they said, "Thank you, God, that sister is perfect tomorrow." The next day that child was healed—there wasn't the sign of a cold, and these two little brothers simply gave thanks.*

The brothers trusted and believed their prayers powerful enough to improve their sister's condition. They did their best. They prayed, believing. That is all any of us is called to be and do—our best.

We do our best to remember and accept: "There Is Only One Life"—our perfect T.O.O.L.

—*Published in the May 2014* Science of Mind *magazine*

# Ready for Love and Learning

*I am ready for love, the joy and the pain...*
*I am ready for love...*
*Here with an offering of my voice, my eyes, my soul, my mind.*
*Tell me what is enough, to prove I am ready for love.*

— India.Arie, "Ready for Love"

Yes, sister India, I am ready for a universal lovefest, yearning for us to be more patient, considerate, accepting, and loving to ourselves and each other.

And yet, too often, I am ensnared in disappointment, judgment, and criticism. I harp on all the bad manners, disdain, and vitriol that are becoming omnipresent in our media and public exchanges. When did it become en vogue to be racist, sexist, and overtly prejudiced?

I want to shout from the rooftops, "Friends, please stop! No more clicking on 'Share' to forward what never should have been recorded in the first place." While I accept that these social media posts may be someone's reality, I choose not to engage in them for my own entertainment. And even as I write this, I am aware that I, too, am contributing—through my own judgment and disdain—to the overall mean-spiritedness proliferating on social media and on public display.

But I thought I was ready. What right do I, or any of us, have to establish what is acceptable for another to record and share? My reaction exposes that I focus more on the problem than the solution, fueling a fire already on the verge of burning out of control. This may have been my way of projecting unresolved anger, unhealed pain, or an unwillingness to honor our oneness and practice seeing myself as the other.

Whatever it is, I am still ready. Ready to learn, as the Apostle Paul suggests in 2 Corinthians 5:7, to walk by faith and not by sight. I am ready to release what lies behind and stretch toward what is ahead. The trainer in me still believes that "the best way to learn something is to teach it."

—Published in the September 2014 Science of Mind *magazine*

# Reframe, Repot, and Bloom

As we expand our concept of self, we can begin to see ourselves as more capable, better able to negotiate life. In truth, when we honor our past, we realize we are more challenge-able, break-up-able, rejection-able, no-balance-in-the-bank-able than we ever imagined we could be.

It is up to us to know ourselves: Who am I truly? What am I made of, and what am I capable of? In this way, we can better discern when we have outgrown our current consciousness and know which of our relinquished dreams and soured visions are worth resuscitating through a focused spiritual practice.

Much like the slow death of a plant, it happens in full view. No more blossoms or new growth, the life and color gradually fades from leaves, and the leaves wither and drop off. It seems evident that our plant (dream) is dead or dying.

When we remove the plant from its pot, we find the roots tied, knotted, crowded, and turning in on themselves. We realize there is no room in this pot for the plant to live, grow, and be. If we do not repot our plant, death is imminent.

We are like potted plants that have outgrown the consciousness of our past. However, we can reawaken our shriveled, comatose dreams. We must begin our spiritual repotting to expand our bandwidth—in mind, heart, and spirit—to receive, accept, and experience our desired visions and dreams. Something more can manifest as we let go of our judgment about how it has been and develop the emotional intelligence and muscle to look beyond the past and claim an expanded future.

What if all of our experiences, even the ones we believe never should have happened, have come to light our path beyond our former sense of self? Reframing the past offers ideal opportunities to expand beyond our disappointment with what was and embrace our greater-yet-to-be. Instead of struggling against our perceptions of the past, we can practice staying present and releasing the fear that had us trying to pray away any possibility of a similar experience.

—*Published in the October 2014* Science of Mind *magazine*

# Mind Your Mind

Recently, I had a horrendous experience. Suffice to say, I was a victim at the effect of a master villain, held in circumstances that had me running from bad to worse and back again. Although I contrived clever workarounds, pled exceptions, and offered contingencies, my feeble struggle to free myself from this tyranny—like thrashing about in a straitjacket—served to further entangle me.

Then I remembered a favorite Albert Einstein quote: "No problem can be solved from the same level of consciousness that created it." What a wake-up call! I realized I had been self-identifying with the problem, camped in the "valley of the shadow of death," and actively courting fear. All this, from a few moments of terrifyingly negative self-talk and dizzying circular mind activity.

Much like the prodigal son in Luke 15, at the lowest point of his despair, I, too, came to myself. I awakened, interrupted the negative transmissions to my subconscious mind, and began imagining and transmitting a new vision and outcome.

In coming to myself, I remembered who (and whose) I am and engaged the power in the present moment. In a word, I was *mindful*. It is in mindfulness that we begin to notice. We become aware that we have taken a wrong turn and have begun sliding down a dangerously slippery slope.

Mindfulness helps us gain the presence, courage, and adeptness to slow our downward trajectory and deftly shift our intention. Once we shift, withdrawing our attention from our negative self-talk, we can be more available to this moment and infinitely more effective.

Mindfulness grounds and focuses our energy in such a way that our experience of life and our desired outcomes meld in perfect alignment. The past loses its power and seductive pull as we cease wasting time fretting about it and arguing for our regrets.

Mindfulness is an invitation to be fully present to this precious now. Maybe that's what Rumi had in mind when he wrote, "Out beyond ideas of wrong-doing and right-doing, there is a field. I'll meet you there."

Are you coming?

—*Published in the March 2015* Science of Mind *magazine*

# Heel Your Mind

I marvel at the synergistic relationship well-trained dogs appear to have with their owners. When these proactive owners call their dogs, their dogs respond immediately, physically attuned, ears poised. By contrast, untrained dogs and their often-frazzled owners appear to have an entirely different and rather dysfunctional relationship.

Owners of untrained or poorly trained dogs struggle to gain cooperation from their pets. These dogs seem bent on doing as they fancy, regardless of their owners' pleading and shouting for a different behavior.

Although we prefer to envision our minds as focused on and attuned to our highest and best, too often our minds behave more like insufficiently trained dogs—chasing cars, humping legs, chewing precious objects—than the focused guidance systems we require for living our best lives.

We naively expect our mind to respond to our wisest suggestions, even though we have not trained it to do so. Just as a dog who has never been trained to respond to the command "Heel!" is unlikely to shift its focus from whatever it was doing pre-command, likewise our human mind, engaged in its monkey-mind machinations, continues to whirl with thoughts of doubt and fear, even as we shout commands to correct course.

In the same way we call our pets to quiet and stillness, we benefit by doing the same with our mind. Mindfulness is the solution.

Dog whisperer Cesar Milan's clarity and guidance regarding dogs may also be applied to our minds. He says, "Many dogs grow up without rules or boundaries. ... Dogs naturally respect 'invisible boundaries' much more so than man-made ones. They set invisible limitations for one another all the time by using energy and body language. But you must take the time and patience to reinforce the rules until your puppy internalizes them. ... They're actually looking for you to be the pack leader. We're the only species who follow unstable leaders."

Milan's guidance calls us to clarity and dominion. None of us want unstable leadership directing our minds. Let's set an intention to be consistent in focusing our power and stay aware that whatever we reinforce is what we will ultimately demonstrate.

Holmes told us, "The trained mind is far more powerful than the untrained mind." He also suggested, "Prepare your mind to receive the best that life has to offer."

—*Published in the March 2016* Science of Mind *magazine*

# An Inner Renovation

*Somebody told us to love one another*
*Quiet the mind and be still.*
*Now is the time to believe who you are*
*And marry your soul with your will.*

— Gina Breedlove, "The Healers"

Who do you think you are?! Whether you ask yourself this question or sense it in another's reaction, do your best to respond from authentic self-awareness. Of necessity, love requires acceptance. We are unable to truly love ourselves as "one another" until we include and demonstrate acceptance of self. Your current sense of who you are informs your present experiences. We can accept Gina Breedlove's lyrical invitation to "quiet the mind and be still" as a call to mindfulness and authentic self-awareness—our gateway to transformation.

Transformation is akin to employing a full renovation of our intent and discernment. In this inner renovation, we endeavor to upgrade our capacity to be real, engage our sense of innocence, and expand our expression of our authentic self. Similar to a typical building renovation, space must first be created for our emerging vision. To this end, we will be required to deconstruct our erroneous thinking and release the doubts and fears obstructing direct access to our authentic essence.

A specialized tool belt is required for our inner renovation. The essential tools are forgiveness, trust, love, compassion, integrity, and courage. We must commission each of these principles in service to our new design for living.

As we renovate, we upgrade our consciousness—our sense of everything—especially who and how we think we are, what appears to be happening in every situation, and the meaning we assign to it. This is all transformed, and as we begin opening ourselves to the fullness of life, healing happens. We begin to discern and more consistently access the Divine order in our universe. Transformation is well underway.

Who do you think you are?! Affirm your IS-ness from your inner wisdom and divine sense of self. Courageously declare the most empowering affirmation your consciousness can grasp. Give voice to the truth of your being—"believe who you are."

This is a call to authenticity. Reveal your authentic self. Just do you—be the *real* you—in expressing the *I am*.

—*Published in the May 2016* Science of Mind *magazine*

# Clear Sight

*I can see clearly now, the rain is gone,*
*I can see all obstacles in my way.*
*Gone are the dark clouds that had me blind.*
*It's gonna be a bright, bright, sun-shiny day.*

— Johnny Nash, "I Can See Clearly Now"

I suspect that Southern California readers would understand better than most how their San Francisco Bay Area cousins prayed in earnest for rain, and yet feel more irritated and inconvenienced by our recent showers than we feel grateful. And of course, we become a virtual choir, passionately singing all the verses of Johnny Nash's "I Can See Clearly Now."

Even as I begrudged the rain, I simultaneously imagined a more lush and lovely garden. The rain ensured that the barren areas would now teem teeming with life. Today, there are new seedlings of mint, flowers, vines, and weeds, the essence of which obviously had been there all along, hidden in plain sight. I see it all so clearly now.

The human imagination is a source of great power. Engaging it is our essential role in the creative process. All possibilities are accessible to us by clarifying our desired outcomes in mind, attuning to the imagined outcome as if our desire already is manifest, and then fully engaging our sensory perceptions to believe and *imagine it into being.*

"I Can See Clearly Now" reminds us of the importance of an expectant state of mind and resolute receptivity. It invites us to examine how and where we direct our focus. When our plans are thwarted, we literally can feel as if a door slammed closed to our good. If we let our disappointment seep in and paralyze us, we are likely to be blind to any doors held open for us.

Genevieve Behrend, French-born author and teacher of Mental Science, puts it simply: "My mind is a center of Divine operation. I will not be discouraged."

This can be our truth, too. We do not have to come undone by the rains or storms, the trials or tribulations. We can instead be steady in focusing our inner vision and employing our imagination to actively live in our desired outcome. The shift occurs first in mind, then as our experience. Today can indeed be "a bright sun-shiny day."

—*Published in the March 2017* Science of Mind *magazine*

# Affirm It So

*The person who dares to fling their thought out into
Universal Intelligence, with the assurance of one who realizes
their divine nature and its relation to the Universe—
and dares to claim all there is—will find an ever-creative good
at hand to aid them. God will honor their request. To the soul
that knows its own divinity, all else must gravitate.*

— Ernest Holmes

Sometimes, I fling my thought into Universal Intelligence like a superhero and then bask in the manifestation of my consciousness. And sometimes I require assistance in establishing and maintaining the assurance of one who realizes their divine nature. In either case, I engage affirmations to help remind me of my divinity.

The key to success is repetition. Just saying it is not enough. We must say it *with feeling*, over and over, until our subconscious believes it. Here's the secret: Put it to music. I am known for putting a song that inspires me on repeat and playing it for weeks at a time. I intentionally do this until the lyrics morph into empowering affirmations, turbocharged by the melodies on their ride into my subconscious.

It is similar to the way many of us learned our ABCs. The tune made it easier for us to keep the letters in the correct order and often revealed that we knew more of the letters than we had consciously committed to memory.

My current musical affirmation comes from "You Are the Universe," by Siedah Garrett and Andrew Levy. My favorite lyrics are an antidote to self-doubt:

> *You're a winner, so, do what you came here for*
> *The secret weapon isn't secret anymore*
> *You're a driver, never passenger in life*
> *And when you're ready, you won't have to try, 'cause*
> *You are the Universe*
> *And there ain't nothin' you can't do*
> *If you conceive it, you can achieve it*
> *That's why I believe in you, yes, I do…*

The lyrical affirmations in this song remind me of how life gets to be the way it is and the consciousness required to shift. They also provide me the perfect inspiration for such a time as this.

Under the influence of such an empowering message, I find myself in the divine gravitational field where I believe in me *and* I believe in you.

—*Published in the August 2017* Science of Mind *magazine*

# #MeToo: A Powerful Movement

*#MeToo is essentially about survivors supporting survivors, and it's really about community healing and community action. Although we can't define what healing looks like for people, we can set the stage and give people the resources to have access to healing. And that means legitimate things like policies and laws that change to support survivors.*

— Tarana Burke, founder of the #MeToo movement

Recently, we saw and heard many of our sisters, no longer willing to cower and live in doubt of their own innate power and divine presence, give voice to their truth. We are shifting, evolving beyond the erroneous belief that any abuse we experienced, negation we've been through, or however inappropriately we've been treated can alter the truth of who we are. This shift is our metamorphosis from feeling invisible, damaged, devalued, unloved, unheard, disbelieved, and distrusted to the truth—an abiding sense of I AM worthy, valued, divine, and loved.

Often a key mindset and threat against giving voice to #MeToo is that "no one will believe me." It is the definitive devaluation of your word, experience, truth, and self-worth. The ultimate threat is that if you stand up, if you lift your voice and tell, if you dare resist, your situation will only get worse. This is the historical threat levied on all oppressed humans as a means to entrap, enslave, and impede them from realizing, expressing, and living in their divinity.

Holmes wrote, "As we bring ourselves to a greater vision, we induce a greater concept and thereby demonstrate more in our experience. ... Little by little, we can unfold our consciousness, through the acquisition of greater and still greater mental equivalents, until at last we shall be made free."

Women whose tongues were stilled now are discovering and reclaiming their voices, unbridling their deferred courage, and declaring their truths. These women often experience meeting themselves for the first time as whole, capable, and worthy of standing for themselves.

We had our power all the time. It is never too late to stand in the truth and speak your word, illuminating and expanding your individual experiences of the I AM.

—*Published in the March 2018* Science of Mind *magazine*

# *Igniting Mental Conviction*

*The truth is that every day offers opportunities to allow some light to shine through the cracks of the wall called our belief system into the unexplored rooms where our spiritual nature dwells, waiting patiently for us to enter and be more of who we have come here to be.*

— Dennis Merritt Jones

Recently, I supported a dear friend during a serious health challenge. My friend was tremendously well-versed in the ramifications of her diagnosis and prognosis. So when I visited her in the hospital, she knew all too well that her condition was potentially life-threatening. Because she is also a student of Science of Mind, she was thoroughly receptive to spiritual mind treatment (or prayer) and choosing a more desirable alternative to the current medical prognosis.

As Religious Scientists, we are blessed to know that the power of Mind, when fully engaged, is a magnet, drawing us ever toward our good while pulling our good to us. This is how we create our lives—it is done unto us as we believe. The power of prayer, especially spoken as spiritual mind treatment, engages and enlivens the power of Mind.

What began as my suggestion that my friend use her extensive knowledge of the human body to help her envision perfect circulation, perfect assimilation, and perfect elimination became a spontaneous prayer treatment in the emergency intensive care unit. As I began speaking from a place of "what I know for sure" about Divine Love expressing as her health, I realized I was also announcing the goodness of God. I had begun praying in earnest.

With conviction, I declared her ever-present wellness and the divine flow of health and vitality within her whole, perfect, and complete body, knowing that the abiding principle of health and wellness is not restricted by medical history, diagnosis, prognosis, or precedent, aided in surrendering doubt and uncertainty. Although I do not recall the specific words I spoke, I know they ignited the power of Mind, accessed the field of infinite possibility, and put my friend and me on notice that we were fully empowered to envision and claim a vibrant, healthy alternative.

And *claim it* we did. I give thanks that all is well.

—Published in the September 2018 Science of Mind *magazine*

# Speaking Truth to Doubt

*The source of all creation is pure consciousness ... pure potentiality seeking expression from the un-manifest to the manifest. And when we realize that our true self is one of pure potentiality, we align with the power that manifests everything in the universe.*

— Deepak Chopra

Recently, one of my favorite young adults phoned me from college, lamenting about impending midterms and projects due simultaneously. This young man—a bright and promising student who is on a scholarship and the dean's list—was berating himself and doubting his well-established academic success, proven intellect, and demonstrated abilities. He was knee-deep in self-flagellation, feeling defeated by assignments not yet due and denying his current capacity to succeed.

I chose to see beyond his perception and instead envisioned him awaking to his spiritual magnificence and discovering the full creative power of his thought, and I told him so. I reframed the demoralizing situation he described into a divine demonstration in which he was empowered to realize his personal power and the ability to create his life cohesively within a world that works for everyone. This vision was a blessing to both of us.

It fit perfectly with a quote from Holmes I previously shared with him: "The range of our possibilities at the present time does not extend far beyond the range of our present concepts. As we bring ourselves to a greater vision, we induce a greater concept and thereby demonstrate more in our experience."

Yes! He and I collaborated on shifting his present concept from defeat to seeing himself as a whole, perfect, and complete being, successfully finishing his junior year. My work was to remind him of the basics—the abiding truth—and his work was to remember the same. I declared the truth, and he gradually released his doubt and began embracing an expanded sense of pure potentiality.

He acknowledged and owned responsibility for his current state of mind as a direct consequence of this *being done unto him as he believed*. He chose again. He began affirming, "Divine love and divine truth gracefully clear the way for increased comprehension and success in all my classes and studies." And so it is.

—Published in the January 2019 Science of Mind *magazine*

# Born to Be Free

*I had reasoned this out in my mind—there was one of two things
I had a right to, liberty or death. If I could not have one,
I would have the other, for no man should take me alive.*

— Harriet Tubman

Both *The Slave Narratives* and common culture chronicle that Mother Harriet Tubman, in anticipating she was to be sold into the Deep South by her enslaver, instead escaped under cover of night, engaged the Underground Railroad, and deftly navigated the treacherous route to freedom. Preceding her escape, something happened in her awareness—a trigger event—shifting her vision of what was possible and what was hers to be and do.

In hopeless situations, some people suddenly seem to be able to do what was thought impossible and see what had been invisible. What if it were true for us as well, that crisis illuminates opportunities previously hidden? We could begin to imagine the steps to unchain ourselves from our past and present circumstances so as to realize a more desirable future. We could discern a way through the challenge rather than remaining chained in fear, doubting our access to freedom.

Sometimes, "chained in fear" is a metaphor. However, it was literal for Amanda Berry, a teenager who was kidnapped in 2003 and imprisoned until 2013. On May 6, 2013, Berry attempted escape, gained the assistance of a neighbor, broke through the front door, and emancipated herself and her six-year-old daughter. Her escape also freed two other young women held captive in the same home.

Her story and Mother Harriet's legacy remind me that, in truth, we are more empowered than we typically realize.

We often require a trigger event to realize and illuminate how we might do what we previously thought was impossible. Holmes wrote, "We have a greater degree of choice and freedom than we have ever realized. In some way or other, by some inward compulsion and conviction, we feel that we are born to be free and happy, and we ever desire to seek this larger life."

Mother Harriet, Holmes, and Berry remind us that we, too, have a right to unchain and be free.

—Published in the July 2020 *Science of Mind* magazine

# A House Divided Against Itself

I marvel at the timeless wisdom and evolutionary vision of Abraham Lincoln, who, in 1858, as a candidate for the Illinois legislature, said, "A house divided against itself cannot stand. I believe this government cannot endure permanently half slave and free. I do not expect the Union to be dissolved. I do not expect the house to fall, but I do expect it will cease to be divided. It will become all one thing or all the other."

This is essential guidance for such a time as this. As we release 2020 and launch 2021, we are at a similar crossroads in consciousness. We cannot simultaneously be enslaved to tyranny and be free to thrive.

Rev. Dr. Will Coleman interpreted Jesus's response to Nicodemus in John 3:3 as, "Unless one is born from above, in consciousness, one cannot see the new possibility—the new reality—in the midst of the status-quo regime."

This resonated, in large part, because I recognize this same principle in Holmes's writings when he said, "We shall find a better God when we shall have arrived at a higher standard for man. If God is to interpret Himself *to* man, He must interpret Himself *through* man. And the Spirit can give no gift that we do not accept."

Those who know the truth are prepared to accept the gift and are called to practice love, compassion, acceptance, and inclusion.

As truth-seekers, we know this notion of us being a house divided against itself is always an inside job. Knowing is not enough. Declaring is insufficient. We can, however, align our intent and impact to more beneficial outcomes.

It is up to us—*all* of us—who embrace New Thought and ancient wisdom truth teachings. If we are committed to calling forth a world that works for everyone, we cannot afford to operate as a house divided.

We have too many crises and much healing to do. It is time to harness our wisdom and fortitude to consistently engage and invest our thoughts, words, and deeds in a world that works for everyone.

—*Published in the January 2021* Science of Mind *magazine*

# *We Believe in Freedom*

*Until the killing of Black men, Black mothers' sons, becomes as important to the rest of the country as the killing of a White mother's sons, we who believe in freedom cannot rest.*

— Ella Baker

Bernice Johnson Reagon, founder of Sweet Honey in the Rock, used this quote to write "Ella's Song" in honor of the life and work of Civil Rights hero Ella Baker. Although the song was released in 1988, it foretold the "Wall of Moms" we saw in Portland, Oregon, in the summer of 2020. These mainly White, mostly suburban moms positioned themselves between the police and the throngs protesting the murder of George Floyd.

This song came to mind when a jury found Derek Chauvin guilty of murdering George Floyd on April 20, 2021. This news sparked a full range of emotions and triggered deep generational trauma for me and many others. This is still a tender time for many, and our tears continue to flow into the hollow wells of our would-be allies' silence and could-be co-conspirators' absence.

What is it we do not understand about the Jesus's declaration in Matthew 22:39? "You shall love your neighbor as yourself," invites us to tune into and honor the guidance of Divine Love. Those moms knew resting was not an option and modeled that genuine "thoughts and prayers" are best expressed as full conviction and active commitment when they put their safety on the line.

Last summer, millions took to the streets as co-conspirators for justice—the right use of spiritual law—and affirmed, "Black lives matter!" Because they believe in freedom, they protested police violence, the increasing militarization of police, and municipalities' ambivalence toward violence against their most vulnerable citizens.

No, we cannot yet rest. We must commit to transforming and calling forth a new, more inclusive, and humane experience for everyone *now*. It is time for us to be the change and embody a global vision: to redesign and rededicate the inequitable systems that fail to ensure the safety and freedom for us to breathe and live full, productive lives while Black. Yes, we who believe in freedom must invest in a world that works for all.

—*Published in the July 2021* Science of Mind *magazine*

# Even in the Movies

*If thought is acted on by the creativity of Mind to produce results according to your belief, then you surely do have the power to become the master of your own affairs and to possess those good conditions you desire.*

— Ernest Holmes

This quote from Holmes stirred up a mental revival of three of my favorite films, beginning with this quote from *What the Bleep Do We Know!?*: "If everything I perceive is based on what I already know, how will I ever perceive anything new? If I never perceive anything new, how will I change?" This film posits that our future is just possible timelines—until we choose. And choose we must. Otherwise, we are stuck in an eddy of historic knowing, living in the past.

In *Tomorrowland,* more people believed in the doomsday scenario based on an algorithm of despair than in the probability of a vibrant prosperous life. Therefore, the doomsday future was all they could foresee.

However, visionaries can see beyond into the field of infinite possibility. A young character in this film did not believe and refused to accept the doomsday projection as inevitable. Her belief in a positive future generated a higher vibration. Her unique view—her mental equivalent—awakened a positive future potential. It was a future that, before she energized it, was not a known or viable option.

These scenes corroborate how we create our reality, how what we believe sets our framework for calling forth new life.

As you may recall, the movie *Back to the Future* also illustrated that the future is just a potential. It fluctuates in mind and collective consciousness until it manifests as the present moment. As Doc Brown told Marty McFly, "Your future hasn't been written yet. No one's has. Your future is whatever you make it. So make it a good one."

This is for us to realize as well. We, too, can go back to the future of our choosing, and, as Holmes suggested, harness our power to be, do, and have the good conditions we desire.

—Published in the November 2021 *Science of Mind* magazine

# Burst of Creativity

*There is a stream of relentless Power running through every one of us. Its outlet is in the mental and emotional thought, imagination, and desire that moves us at bottom. Creative desire is that quality and that energy that permit us to soar above the stress and strain of daily life and to see the happy ending. There is Something moving through us that has no end, that has no limit to its depth.*

— Dr. Daniel L. Morgan

I testify, with some trepidation, that I have only recently discerned the direct correlation between my experience in darkness and the divine burst of creativity awaiting me on the other side. This revelation came on the tail end of a deep, dark night of the soul.

I felt betrayed, and my heart felt broken. I was triggered, in a bad way. Just as the weight of race consciousness often burdens those of us who are still at the effect of unhealed trauma, I felt as if I had been knocked off my center—the centered awareness I rely on. The happy ending evaded me.

I am not certain why I entertained this for as long as I did. I do know it ultimately blessed me. Even as my heart ached and I seemed to spin deeper into doubt, I truly desired a positive shift. I spoke a prayer of love and blessing, affirming the highest and best for all. I called forth the Presence and demonstration of the divine creative process.

There is much about these dark experiences that I cannot explain. However, I do know it is done unto me as I believe. The more I surrender, believe, accept, and open myself to imagine more positive outcomes, the more I directly access my inner power, experience a sense of freedom, and find the wherewithal to soar above the stress and strain.

This was such an adventure in faith and a simultaneous invitation to engage my stream of power with the Divine. I did what Toni Morrison suggested: "If you want to fly, you must give up the things that weigh you down."

—Published in the April 2022 Science of Mind magazine

## *Better and Better and Better*

During Supreme Court Justice Ketanji Brown Jackson's Senate confirmation hearing, Senator Cory Booker's remarks moved me to tears—tears of joy and sadness. I identified with his sense of our collective body of affairs, our circuitous route to the full protection of civil rights for all Americans, and our capricious commitment to human rights. In his impassioned remarks, he also said, "This country is getting better and better and better." It's true! Even as we watch our struggle to hear, understand, accept, and bless each other play out on the world stage, I believe we simultaneously expand our consciousness, maturing and becoming ever more aware of our individual and collective impact.

Booker's declaration reminded me of the French psychologist and pharmacist, Émile Coué, who in the early 1900s introduced a popular method of psychotherapy and self-improvement based on optimistic auto-suggestion. As he filled prescriptions, he included this affirmation, "Day by day, in every way, I'm getting better and better." This affirmation was an autosuggestion, intended for daily application, to aid in the patient's healing.

I continue to nurture an ever-higher vision of us living in a world that works for all. This *all* comprises the entire body of our affairs. The word *body* in Science of Mind is the objective manifestation of the invisible principle of life. The physical universe is the body of God, the manifestation of the invisible principle of all life. Our physical being is the body of the unseen human/principle.

Our transformation, the healing of our body—our body of affairs—begins in mind. Coué was known for supporting his patients' healing by declaring the efficacy of the treatment and including a positive note with each prescription to establish successful healing in mind. He is credited with discovering the placebo effect.

There is no question that the body and our affairs respond to our thoughts and feelings. We can discern the specific mental attitudes and equivalents to every physical manifestation. We experience how joyful thoughts foster joy, thoughts of peace produce more peaceful interactions, and how anxiety-producing our fearful thoughts are.

Knowing our thoughts are prescriptive to our body of affairs, I invoke Romans 12:2: "Be ye transformed by the renewing of your mind."

—*Published in the June 2022* Science of Mind *magazine*

# Mother Nature

*Look at a tree, a flower, a plant. Let your awareness rest upon them, how still they are, how deeply rooted in Being. Allow nature to teach you stillness.*

— Eckhard Tolle

Three times a week, in the early morning, I willingly enter another realm. I walk around Lake Merritt in the center of Oakland, California. Lake Merritt is a tidal lagoon and home to the United States' oldest designated wildlife refuge, dating back to 1870. This regular walk is my salvation. The lake has become an alternate universe for me. It is here I observe animate energy moving throughout the grounds and water, and I invite Mother Nature to teach me essential lessons about her life. I find nature to be a creative teacher for my willing student.

Lake Merritt teems with life. Ducks, mallards, geese, pelicans, herons, and pigeons galore feed on the insects, mussels, and fish in the lake, which is surrounded by an abundance of beautiful trees, plants, and flowers. I watch a variety of dogs engage with their walkers. There also are several unhoused encampments, and often the trash and debris accumulate faster than the city workers can manage. The city workers and those completing community service do an admirable job, and nature includes all these players—every one—in my curriculum. I am becoming ever more adept at recognizing and acknowledging the face of God and discerning the Divine Presence in all life.

My lake experience continues to open my mind and heart to notice and even seek additional evidence of divine order everywhere. Recently, I read about dolphins rubbing against corals. The scientists looked at which corals the dolphins rubbed against and the effect it had on both the dolphins and the coral reef. They determined the abrasive action of the dolphins scraping against the coral activates polyps within the coral, and the coral exudes a mucus containing antibacterial, anti-oxidative, and hormonal properties. The dolphins self-medicated by rubbing up against the coral. It seems this mucus healed their skin.

I am grateful to Mother Nature for these most recent lessons on how genuine, loving interest reveals the divine circle and order of life. I can't wait to see what else I notice and learn from nature.

—*Published in the August 2022* Science of Mind *magazine*

# Rest to Replenish

Although I have an authentic desire for a world that works for everyone, the one I created did not work for me. This is evidenced by how I responded to stress over the last three years. At the height of the Covid pandemic, I isolated to a fault. I also internalized my dementia patient's words and actions, harbored anxiety about her care, denied my grief, and consigned my health and heart to stress and anxiety. I constantly obsessed about whether I was doing enough, wondering, "Am I really doing everything I can?"

According to Shawn Ginwright, Ph.D., "Wise farmers let the soil rest for a season, knowing that resting the soil would ultimately produce better crops. Resting the soil regenerates nutrients, replenishes important minerals, and restores soil quality. We should learn from these wise farmers and prioritize the need to replenish. We all have the right to restore ourselves. ... Replenishing ourselves is the only real way to make the deep change we need in our world."

I am writing this from Ocho Ríos, Jamaica. This is my first vacation since 2019, and it is a step forward in my self-care. On the flight to Jamaica, my seatmate offered her cautionary tale of how having breast cancer and a mastectomy changed her relationship with work, rest, and relaxation.

My inciting incident was a recent arterial fibrillation episode, the consequence of a deadly cocktail of stress, anxiety, grief, and exhaustion. That concoction landed me in the emergency room. When they admitted me, I took note and wisely wrote myself a prescription for self-care. (Note: Self-care is collective care. My spiritual community is better off when I am rested.)

I came to Jamaica to sleep and relax on the beach, and my time away was restorative. Google the importance of rest and sleep, and you will find both are key to our mental, emotional, and physical well-being. Although there are still stressors in my life, I feel more attentive and committed to my physical, mental, and emotional health. Making restorative self-care a priority helps me make the deep change required to live my fullest life.

I am willing to change and set a new example. Are you?

—Published in the June 2023 Science of Mind *magazine*

## SECTION 6

# *Gratitude*

## FROM THE INSIDE OUT

*When we focus on our gratitude,
the tide of disappointment goes out
and the tide of love rushes in.*

— Kristin Armstrong

## Our Gift of Ruin

Last summer, I read Elizabeth Gilbert's blog in which she examines the gift of ruin, and it continues to fuel my sense of gratitude for my darkest nights and worst life experiences.

Gilbert wrote, "Change, to put it simply, is the suck. Nobody wants to do it—not real change, not soul change, not the painful molecular change required to truly become who you need to be. Nobody ever does real transformation for fun. ...You do it only when your back is so far against the wall that you have no choice anymore."

I am reminded of chief *Inside Edition* correspondent and former CNN anchor Jim Moret, who experienced a familiar trajectory of transformation.

He perceived that he was worth more dead than alive and felt that "the real prospect of losing everything you have worked your entire life to achieve is devastating and utterly demoralizing." During his dark night of the soul, he plotted suicide as the solution to his financial troubles.

Even when we descend to the lowest place in our life, as we crash and burn, we simultaneously are empowered to make choices that mirror the caterpillar's urge to gorge until it is ultimately enveloped in its cocoon. Inside the cocoon—in the dark, mysterious goo—is where the full transformation takes place. Moret said he emerged from his goo once he began practicing gratitude and forgiveness.

Change demands that we release the beautiful butterfly previously concealed within our "caterpillar-ness." Our new expression is totally inaccessible until we transform through the goo of ruin. Although the imaginal cells of the caterpillar contain the DNA of the butterfly, inside the cocoon, the caterpillar must dissolve into goo-soup before it can fly.

In our human version, when we are "in the goo," we are not who we have been, and we are not yet who we are becoming. Even though we may first identify the goo as our ruin, it is actually our blessing.

Gilbert wrote, "You will crawl and bawl until eventually you are standing, finally, on your own two feet in your own shower of light ... [as] the person you never would have been had you never met your own worst darkness face to face. And that is the gift that ruin offers us." Give thanks!

— *Published in the November 2014* Science of Mind *magazine*

# A Gift of Love and Forgiveness

This has been a challenging year [2014] for many. Some are reeling from numerous reports of terrorism and horrendous acts. Even as we work to "change our thinking, change our lives," we sense the need to go deeper in order to change our reality. As we bring closure to this year and open up to 2015, I wonder how we can clean up our collective act and set our lives right.

Let's consider *Ho'oponopono*, the ancient Hawaiian prayer of forgiveness and reconciliation. It is defined as "mental cleansing—to put to rights; to put in order or shape, correct, revise, adjust, amend, regulate, arrange, rectify, tidy up, make orderly or neat."

The definition reminds me of an infomercial: "It heals everything! But wait—there's more! The following mantra surpasses the effectiveness of any other cleaning tool on the market to 'put to rights' and truly improve life."

Often referred to as self-cleansing, the Ho'oponopono mantra, "I love you, I'm sorry, please forgive me, thank you," helps us:

- Be and express authentic love for the Divine in and as *all*.
- Acknowledge and apologize for anything in consciousness and vibration, known or unknown, that contributed to the situation.
- Forgive ourselves and release the situation to be healed.
- Give thanks to the Divine, which is the true self.

Dr. Hew Len, co-author of *Zero Limits*, teaches that "total responsibility for your life means that everything in your life—simply because it is in your life—is your responsibility."

This means all that stuff in the news you don't like is for you to heal, from the inside out. At its core, Ho'oponopono calls us to love the Divine as ourselves. It is the way to initiate a positive shift in our lives. In loving more fully, we simultaneously release within ourselves whatever created the problem.

We are the sole creators of our entire existence. As Holmes wrote, "[Man] must accept the responsibility for his choices, because inexorable Law will create his experiences according to his choices."

We have the power to create whatever world we want to live in, and we can do it by engaging four simple phrases from a consciousness of 100 percent responsibility—for everyone's actions, not only our own. The problem is not with our external reality. It is within us and up to us to change.

*— Published in the December 2014* Science of Mind *magazine*

# My New Vision

The benefit of a new vision is commensurate with our willingness to see that we had access to it all along. Often we find ourselves, in our new awareness, asking, "How could I have been so blind?", wondering how we missed the obvious ... again.

We are left to search for a cure, something to permanently extricate us from our former perception of situations past, present, and anticipated. *A Course in Miracles* (ACIM) teaches that nothing we see means anything; everything has only the meaning we assign to it. Our society assigns significance and added meaning to skin and hair color, job titles, nationality, sexual orientation, age, gender, etc. History reveals that life unfolds in a unique (if not peculiar) order; and, in time, some of our intentions and assigned meanings change. We ultimately come to embrace a new vision.

I recall how the United States previously had adversarial relationships with countries with which we are now aligned. I look forward to seeing how and when our new vision of Cuba, for example, will supplant our former political rhetoric.

I rejoice whenever I hear of family members who, once they realize their beloved son or sister is same-gender loving, embrace a new vision of inclusion.

I shared many tear-filled moments with millions of *Oprah* viewers when her guests included Congressman John Lewis and Elwin Wilson, the man who apologized privately and on national TV for beating Lewis in Selma, Alabama, on Bloody Sunday in 1965.

In another segment, skinheads spewed venom, and then years later returned to apologize, acknowledge their former hatred, and declare a new vision and capacity for acceptance. In these examples, we clearly see a new vision manifesting.

I am grateful for Lesson 21 in *A Course in Miracles*: "I am determined to see things differently." It seems I am beginning to emulate the elders of my youth in my certainty that "in time, even this will change."

Even during such a time as this, I steadfastly embrace a new vision of love, empathy, and acceptance for all people by all of us. After all, this is what we teach and endeavor to practice, and our true nature is love.

— *Published in the May 2015* Science of Mind *magazine*

# *When We Forgive: A New Nation*

*I have blotted out, as a thick cloud, thy transgressions. ...
For, behold, I create new heavens and a new Earth:
and the former shall not be remembered, nor come into mind.*

— Isaiah 44:22

In theory, forgiveness holds that whatever mistakes we made yesterday, through forgiveness, we can create today as "a new Earth." But first, as a nation, we must own our past transgressions—our country's history of violence and forced labor. We are called to acknowledge our errors; release the sorrows, pain, and anger of yesterday; and work toward "a new heaven." The promise is restoration.

Maybe there are lessons in forgiveness and restoration we can learn from South Africa's Truth and Reconciliation Commission. Led by Archbishop Desmond Tutu, the commission's televised proceedings sought healing through telling the authentic truth, required full disclosure of perpetrators' violations, and included survivor stories of harm and grief. Truth and empathetic acceptance of divergent realities worked to expand the capacity for restoration and reconciliation.

Many South Africans who participated seemed to invoke a spirit of reconciliation and radical forgiveness rooted in Ubuntu, an ancient southern African creed that honors our human interdependence: "I am because we are." Indeed, we are responsible for one another, and any action we take against anyone has consequences for us and our lives. This is also found in the ancient truth of Maat: "Now this is the command: Do to the doer to cause that he do thus to you."

It's similar to the Golden Rule: "Do unto others as you would have them do unto you." These are all ethics of reciprocity. Essentially, whatever we perpetrate on each other, we are also doing to ourselves. We are one.

We can engage the spirit of Ubuntu and expand our sense of interdependency and equality between ourselves and others. In *The Book of Forgiving*, Tutu and his daughter, Mpho, write: "Is there a place where we can meet? You and me. The place in the middle. The no man's land. Where we straddle the lines. Where you are right and I am right, too. And both of us are wrong and wronged. Can we meet there? And look for the place where the path begins. The path that ends when we forgive."

— Published in the October 2015 Science of Mind *magazine*

# Choose Gratitude for All Things

*There is a law of gratitude, and if you are to get the results you seek, it is absolutely necessary that you should observe this law.*

— Wallace Wattles, *The Science of Getting Rich*

*A Course in Miracles* defines gratitude as "appreciation for blessings received. The appropriate response to reality and its gifts. An essential aspect of love, which brings joy to those who give it as well as those who receive it."

I declare that gratitude also is a choice. Each of us decides whether and what we appreciate. However, before we can choose to be grateful, we must first acknowledge what is. This practice, when fully engaged, supports us in transmuting our perception of what has been into a lesson in love.

Many of us testify that we've already lived through the worst day(s) of our lives and found that few things ultimately are as bad as we may have thought. We realize that even our worst experiences can be transformed through an attitude of gratitude and the acceptance that all things work together for our good.

A lack of appreciation restricts many people to an experience of lack. Without gratitude, you cannot help but be dissatisfied with things as they are. When you focus on your dissatisfaction with your present state and/or give attention to the mediocre, your mind takes the form of these things.

You can realize mental, emotional, and spiritual recalibration by embracing an attitude of gratitude. When Yeshua, in responding to the call to aid Lazarus in John 11:41–42, said first, "Father, I thank you that you have heard me. And I know that you always hear me," he established a preemptory attitude of gratitude.

This mindset draws us closer into the Source from which all blessings flow, primes our prosperity pump, and expands our capacity to receive.

Let us observe the law and begin to cultivate the habit of being grateful for every good thing that comes to us.

We can also choose to include all things in our gratitude and, like Yeshua, be willing to give thanks first, now, and continuously.

— Published in the November 2015 *Science of Mind* magazine

# No Complaints

*True nonresistance is the surrender of every arrogant attitude
of mind to good and to good alone. Those who have made
this surrender have found real peace of mind, happiness, and wholeness
in the only place it can be found, which is within themselves.*

— Ernest Holmes

I recently read a story about a Zen master named Sono who advised everyone who came to her to declare the following affirmation several times a day, in response to all conditions: "Thank you for everything. I have no complaint whatsoever."

It is said that countless people from everywhere came to Master Sono for healing. They came seeking relief from physical pain, emotional distress, financial dilemmas, and even spiritual liberation.

Regardless of their requests, her guidance was always the same: "Always affirm, 'Thank you for everything. I have no complaint whatsoever.'" While some began to practice as instructed, other responses varied from disappointment and anger to disbelief and contention. The lore is that everyone who sincerely practiced Sono's mantra found peace and healing.

Master Sono's teaching is the conscious use of and union of the powerful principles of gratitude and surrender. Often when we begin to practice surrendering and living in gratitude, we immediately become aware of our disorderly thoughts and contrary thinking.

When we affirm, "Thank you for everything," we find ourselves confronted by all the things we have not been willing to bless and accept in gratitude. As we continue our habitual pattern of complaining, we are, as Mark 3:25 suggests, "a house divided against itself." To heal our house—shift our consciousness—we must surrender our limiting perspectives, doubts, and fears to embrace our greater good. This requires releasing the lesser for the greater—yes, even *that* situation.

We can begin by embracing Master Sono's guidance: In all things, give thanks and surrender all complaining. In biblical terms, this is a classic form of "prayer and fasting." We are called to pray, affirming thanksgiving from an attitude of gratitude, even as we simultaneously fast from complaining. We are encouraged to do this every day, throughout the day. Essentially, we must follow the words in 1 Thessalonians 5:16-18: "Rejoice at all times. Pray without ceasing. Give thanks in everything."

*— Published in the April 2016* Science of Mind *magazine*

## Courage to Forgive

*Everything that happens to me is part of the plan for my awakening, including those challenging events that force me to shift out of my inertia and self-limiting behavior patterns. From the depth of my soul, I call out for growth. I pray to be released from my burdens and to discover and express my gifts. From deep within my pain, I call for peace. From deep within my codependency, I call for the courage and the freedom to be myself, to forgive myself, and to forgive all others.*

— Paul Ferrini

I recently heard commentator Roland Martin address the notion of forgiveness in America and how there seems to be an expectation that African Americans forgive past and recent atrocities committed against them with alacrity. He then cited recent events wherein no such expectation was held when horrible acts were committed against Whites. He asked, "Is there a double standard in America?"

A valid inquiry for some, a risky distraction for me. I cannot afford to begin comparing atrocities. I am still traumatized and triggered by the recent escalating violence in our country and abroad. Instead, I stifle a whine that it's too soon to even speak of forgiveness, as if a timer will buzz when it's time to move from grief and despair to forgiveness and healing.

It would be different if I didn't know better. However, I do know better. Moreover, I was raised with the adage, "When you know better, you are expected to do better."

Today, I also know that forgiveness is our ticket out—out of self-limitation and pain and toward peace, true inner peace. Forgiveness transmutes dissension and clears the way for healing.

We must stretch past our resistance, open our minds and hearts, and engage forgiveness as a healing resource. Our failure to forgive and heal old hurts comes at a cost. In the individual, it lodges in our body temple and manifests as poor health. In our world community, it manifests as systemic bias and hostility. Forgiveness, on any timetable, is vital. This awareness and practice is our ticket to freedom.

— *Published in the October 2016* Science of Mind *magazine*

# Accept and Bless It

*And he ... took the five loaves and two fishes, and looking up to the heaven, he blessed and brake, and gave the loaves to his disciples, and the disciples to the multitude.*

— Matthew 14:19

I have heard it said, "We become what we do." If so, what joy might we realize in being the ones who offer acceptance and blessings as our response to everything?

During a recent Sunday service, after sharing the above scripture, I challenged myself and those gathered to bless everything and everybody, every day. My intent was that we begin to deepen our faith and increase our courage to respond to what appears insufficient now, as if we recognize it as the precursor to an even greater blessing.

Ernest Holmes and Raymond Charles Barker also challenged us: "Have you and I had the faith to bless that which perhaps seemed very small—a loaf of bread and a fish—and to expect it to become multiplied in our experience to such an extent that it would not only bless us but also bless everyone around us?"

Even if our response is, "Not really," or, "Not at all," we can still begin today to accept and bless our experiences in gratefulness.

Responding in gratefulness helps neutralize our doubt and fear. Blessing the perceived problem—whatever it is—helps shift it so we can more fully discern the opportunity it offers. The wise would tell us, "It came to bless you."

Engaging this practice yields immediate positive results. When we accept and bless someone, a situation, or a circumstance, in gratefulness, we anchor our experience of it in gratitude. We can begin by being thankful for our capacity to thrive through the experience, for learning something from it, realizing something we were not aware of prior to the experience. Through this courageous faith-full response, we simultaneously free ourselves to move forward in expanded awareness.

Could it be that we are only one grateful thought away from a world that works for everyone? I challenge us to model the Nazarene's practice: Hold our world in our hearts, accept and bless it, as is, with gratitude, positive expectation, and enthusiasm, and call forth the highest and best for all.

— *Published in the November 2016* Science of Mind *magazine*

# Bless It

*The habit of silently blessing your money as you hand it over is worth cultivating.
Then it carries with it an intangible value that will bring back good.
Learn to bless your bills as you pay them; they indicate the good you have
received and express the faith others have in you.*

— Ernest Holmes

In her book, *The Magic*, Rhonda Byrne lays a foundation of gratitude beneath Holmes's wise advice. Byrne says the secret is in expressing our gratefulness. Central to her theory is Matthew 13:12, and she decodes its cryptic message of prosperity in this way: "Whoever has [gratitude] will be given more, and he will have an abundance. Whoever does not have [gratitude], even what he has will be taken from him."

This makes sense to me and reminds me to honor what my parents taught: Always be grateful. If my behavior did not express gratitude for what I already had been given, I was less likely to receive more of it. Too often, when I pleaded for the latest version of a toy, I was reminded that I'd not taken good care of or demonstrated appreciation for the toys I already had.

Although many of us had similar early coaching, most of us are still not adept at invoking gratitude instead of focusing on what appears to be lacking or accepting an opportunity to complain. There is definitely a great deal we can complain about. Yet, I submit that because our thoughts are magnetic in nature, our complaints attract and draw more complaint-worthy experiences. Likewise, our gratitude and expressions of thanksgiving attract and draw to us comparable opportunities. It seems to be a no-brainer.

The stakes are high, and the secret is gratitude. Byrne suggests we develop a practice of affirming gratitude daily, and she offers specific activities to help us build our gratitude muscle. One activity is to write, "Thank you for all the money I've been given throughout my life" on a sticky note and attach it to a dollar bill. I have done this, and whenever I see it in my wallet, it quashes any thought of struggle or "not enough" and strengthens my resolve to recognize and affirm my blessings. I give thanks for all I've had and that all my needs are met. Happy Thanksgiving.

— *Published in the November 2017* Science of Mind *magazine*

# Gratitude: The Cure for Amnesia

*Giving, I receive, and receiving, I give out again,
thus increasing the Divine bounty that meets me at every turn.*

— Ernest Holmes

Too often we feel stuck in the effect of our challenges, trapped in an eddy of lack. In this state, we seem to be completely unaware of and unavailable to the bountiful good surrounding us everywhere. Essentially, we act as if we are not divinely positioned in the midst of God's bounty *always*. Maybe we're not acting and are instead in a recurring state of amnesia in which our repetitive, limited thinking chokes out the truth of our being, pulls us further into the muck and mire, blinds us to divine reality, and stifles our resilience.

Awareness is the first step out of the eddy. Our opportunity is to somehow create a virtual prodigal son-like scenario in which we come to ourselves and awaken. Once we fully awaken to the ever-present truth, we also realize awaking to this present moment was always an option.

Once awake, we must transmute our challenge into the opportunity it offers. Begin to see the present, with all its difficulties, as a gift. Practice maintaining this clarity of awareness and choose to remain ever grateful, regardless of appearances, even during perceptions of good and bad.

God's bounty is infinite and constantly overflowing to meet our needs. Set an intention to recall as many blessings as you can and sit in profound appreciation and gratitude daily. As you do this, release any belief in lack or limitation. Remember, even a belief in a *maximum abundance* is a limiting belief.

Begin in gratitude. Holmes taught, "Gratitude is not only a virtue, but it is also a part of a practical philosophy of daily life. There is no wiser way of living than to remember every morning what Life has given us and to lift up our thought in thankfulness for every bounty we possess."

Gratitude buoys our spirit and expands our living. Be thankful for the eddy, the amnesia, and the awakening. Express gratitude for everything in your life and watch how you transform.

— *Published in the October 2018* Science of Mind *magazine*

# Willing to Forgive

*Forgive and you shall be forgiven.*

— Luke 6:37

This scripture verse is a clear declaration of freedom. It says to let go, and as you do, you simultaneously will be set free. I know, it sounds too simple, too good to be true. I like to imagine forgiveness as an infomercial: "Forgiveness dissolves negative blocks, mental and emotional burdens from the past and activates the healing power and presence of love."

Hype aside, the requisite order is clear: If we would be forgiven, we must first forgive; and as we forgive, we are forgiven.

The law of forgiveness is mental. It unveils and draws us closer to the whole, perfect, and complete core of our being. However, when we balk and refuse to let go—to forgive—we are, by law, simultaneously refusing to accept our ever-present good. Our resistance and our grudges alienate us and interfere with the divine vibration and flow of good. What we refuse to give, we cannot accept.

We have no right to ask more of the law than we are willing to give of ourselves. Refusing to let go of judgment, condemnation, or retribution leaves us steeped in this negative vibration and perpetuates a negative cycle. None of us is immune to the residual charge or current triggers from negative experiences. Engaging forgiveness helps neutralize our triggers and corrects our perception of the past. Forgiveness offers us direct access to a positive shift in perspectives and the incumbent grace and ease in our new awareness.

During this time of fracture, fear, and divisiveness, I rely on the stories of healing miracles that abound in scripture and in common culture. In these stories, forgiveness releases and heals mental, emotional, spiritual, and physical blockages.

When we release our resistance, rigid opinions, and negative perspectives of an experience or individuals, we open ourselves to experience a positive shift and we gain access, through our new perception, to a higher vibration. Holmes reminds us, "We cannot afford to hold personal animosities or enmities against the world or individual members of society. ... Love alone can beget love."

— *Published in the December 2018* Science of Mind *magazine*

# Miracle Divine

*I now command the multitude of doubts and fears that crowd into my mind to be quiet, while Divine Miracle takes place in my life.*

— Ernest Holmes

During this Lenten season, in which many practice sacrificing the lesser to embrace the greater, I am reminded of the New Testament story of feeding the hungry attributed to Yeshua. Specifically, in the stories of the feeding of the multitude, the people gathered are hungry; the apostles look for food and find "five loaves and two fishes." Yeshua blesses what they gathered, and they feed a multitude.

The lesson of this parable could be the miracle of sharing, that there is more than enough for everyone, and a demonstration of the fair distribution of what we possess. In this social justice scenario, just as in life, Source is never diminished by distribution. For those of us bound by a sense of lack, this demonstration of the power of sharing looks like a miracle instead of a divine truth made manifest.

In 2017, Erika Luckett and I wrote a song, "Miracle Divine." It includes these lyrics:

> *Acceptance spans harmony*
> *And forgiveness is what sets us free.*
> *I let my good become multiplied*
> *As the Divine unfolds in my life*
> *Yes, it is good, it is God, this miracle divine!*

Indeed, it is not until we forgive—let go of the lesser—that we create space to experience the divine miracle of our good multiplied. The multiplication of the loaves and the fishes demonstrates God's grace. The multitude was fed, there was plenty left, nothing went to waste. This was ecologically sound and a divine miracle.

The value of this parable is in our application of the truth revealed: All things are possible. Although many among us remain disenfranchised, homeless, and hungry, this parable promises that our faith in God, acts of forgiveness, and investment in humanity can spawn a miracle divine.

— *Published in the March 2019* Science of Mind *magazine*

# Flow in Faith

*Where there is no faith in the future, there is no power in the present.*

— Halford Luccock

In a recent talk, I enjoyed anthropomorphizing a stream of water and sharing about its purposeful yet circuitous trek to the ocean. The stream wound its way around and through all the large and small boulders and chasms on its way to its intended outcome, and it made it look so easy to do. I marveled at its determination to make its way past all manner of barriers to reach this ultimate goal.

What if we were equally determined to accomplish our goals and realize the greater good awaiting us? Are the obstacles in our way any different than the boulders blocking my stream's path?

Holmes said, "The barriers between you and your greater good are not barriers in themselves. They are things of thought. It is because of this that all things are possible to faith."

Our worries, doubts, fears, complaints, and unwillingness to forgive are like boulders blocking and eddies stifling our flow. They form the countless barriers that cause us to alter our course, risk our safety, and make it increasingly more difficult to reach our goal and accomplish what we set out to do.

While it is always true that the good we seek is also seeking us, we must first believe. Then—in faith, believing—we align ourselves with the good seeking us.

When we do this, we essentially choose a path of nonresistance. This choice empowers us to transmute stumbling blocks into just-in-time stepping stones and make our way safely to our destination. Our faith in our future outcomes strengthens our resolve and endows us with amazing power in the present.

I envision and paint a picture of the stream flowing steadily past all impediments, singing songs of faith, gratitude, and blessings along the way. This consciousness works for us as well. When we are willing to bless our boulders—express gratitude and thanksgiving for every apparent barrier—they dissolve to reveal our highest good, right at hand.

— *Published in the August 2019* Science of Mind *magazine*

# The Unified Game of Life

*If it is happiness that we desire, and we all want to be happy, we pray that joy may come into our life. This is both natural and right.
But so frequently when we are praying for happiness,
we are in an unhappy frame of mind because of our great need.*

— Ernest Holmes

This month we welcome the first day of spring, the vernal equinox. Over the past three months, our daylight hours steadily increased. On March 21, the daylight hours exceed the hours of darkness. This can serve as a metaphor for how our overarching frame of reference can shift from darkness to the presence of light, even in challenging circumstances.

The economy, racism and its stifling constraints and trauma, climate change, plus the poverty and hunger in our midst all help frame and have an impact on what and how many of us think and feel. Our frame of mind is the consciousness from which we live and pray. This frame has everything to do with our receptivity, our sense of what is possible for us, and, thus, the efficacy of our prayers.

There is value in understanding the game of life and developing mastery in how to play it. Owning how life got to be the way it is is key. The truth is, we are already living our best lives, by right of consciousness. On our quest for happiness, we will have opportunities to open to whatever we need to know and experience in our lives. Playing full out requires that we believe and act in alignment with our desired outcome rather than our pressing needs.

We must also give thanks. Thanksgiving is our "get-out-of-jail-free" card. Whatever we appreciate opens to reveal its true purpose. Our sense of appreciation and an attitude of gratitude combine to transform our frame of mind toward embracing our oneness with all humanity.

I invoke Holmes's words: "This is the attitude we should assume, that life holds nothing against us. It desires only our good. … It wants us to play the game of life the way it is supposed to be played—in unity and cooperation with others."

— *Published in the March 2022* Science of Mind *magazine*

# *You Better Work It*

My favorite scripture is Psalm 1:1-3:

1. Blessed is the man that walketh not in the counsel of the wicked, nor standeth in the way of sinners, nor sitteth in the seat of scoffers:
2. But his delight is in the law of Jehovah, and on his law doth he meditate day and night.
3. And he shall be like a tree planted by the streams of water, that bringeth forth its fruit in its season, whose leaf also doth not wither; and whatsoever he doeth shall prosper.

I understand and embrace this scripture as a reminder that my true delight is directly connected to my willingness and ability to place and keep my attention on my intention for the highest and best. I have work to do, and this is my work—our work. Working it means we divert our attention from the condition, tune out race consciousness, laser our focus on our divine intention, and accept any paradox in this effort toward our desired outcome. Divine Law mirrors our faith, and our demonstration must follow.

Psalm 1 illumines our work. It shines light on how we must daily reset our minds, recharge our hearts, and set ourselves on course. Holmes elucidates the wisdom and practicality of this scripture, saying, "The one who wishes scientifically to work out his problems must daily take the time to meditate and mentally treat the condition, no matter what the apparent contradictions may be. He is working silently in the Law, and the Law will find an outlet through his faith in It."

When we meditate on the Law both day and night, we activate our sacred recognition of the Divine. The Law nourishes the tree of our consciousness, rooted in faith, and nurtured by our delight in It. Prosperity, the abundance of all things good, is the fruit we can rightfully expect and anticipate in its season—always in perfect time, space, and form. It works as we work it, when we do our individual and collective work. We have work to do. As the Isley Brothers sang, "I got work to do. Everybody's got work to do. Oh, so much work, baby."

Meditate day and night? You better work it!

— *Published in the September 2022* Science of Mind *magazine*

# Divine Supply

*God is Spirit. Spirit is Substance, and Substance is supply. T
his is the keynote to a realization of the more abundant life,
to the demonstration of success in financial matters.*

— Ernest Holmes

What do we see in our finances? Probably whatever we see in ourselves. However we perceive ourselves, the truth is we must remember that our true nature is love. In practicing the law of love, we come to realize our love is our bounty and the seed of good we sow into the infinite field of divine supply. The resulting experience and life lesson is: The more love we sow, the more love we reap.

In "The Principles of Financial Freedom" (POFF) course, offered by CSL, finance is defined as "the science of money management." It says, "To manage money is to direct or control the use of it, and the way we manage anything is the way we manage everything. Therefore, the way we manage our money tends to be the way we manage our life."

How can we best manage our finances and life? It helps if we:

- Recognize God as Source.
- Accept and embrace money as a spiritual idea, a symbol of divine substance and supply.
- Realize divine supply is unlimited and demonstrated through the power of right-thinking and our use of law.
- Always practice loving-kindness.

Our good is demonstrated through our intentional practice of love and gratitude. God is loving and demonstrating perfectly as us. Just as wellness is our demonstration of the principle of health, prosperity is our demonstration of the principle of abundance.

In POFF we learn, "Financial freedom is the state of mind when money is no longer a restraint in our self-expression." In this state of mind, we recognize the omnipresence of Divine Mind and realize we are all divine beings working out our relationship with life and our finances. We give thanks for divine law manifesting as divine supply in direct response to our beliefs.

Holmes gets the final word: "All good, all substance, all supply, all activity, all opportunity for self-expression are ours now."

*— Published in the October 2022* Science of Mind *magazine*

**SECTION 7**

# Principle and Practice

## FROM THE INSIDE OUT

*You ought to discover some principle, you ought to have some great faith that grips you so much that you will never give it up. Somehow you go on and say, "I know that the God that I worship is able to deliver me, but if not, I'm going on anyhow, I'm going to stand up for it anyway."*

— Rev. Dr. Martin Luther King Jr.

# Look Again

Recently, a friend shared her distress over an e-mail she received. In truth, my friend was the one upset; the e-mail was simply inanimate correspondence in her inbox. This is a recurring theme for many of us. Voicemail, e-mail, and even snail mail appear to be culprits conveying evil or distress. However, in order for us to be upset, we must first be upset-able. In this mode, we prime ourselves to allow almost anything to affect us negatively.

We reap in experience what we sow in consciousness. As it is written in Matthew 12:35, "The good man out of his good treasure bringeth forth good things; and the evil man out of his evil treasure bringeth forth evil things." We become upset, sad, even despondent because we have set a course in a way that "bringeth forth" these experiences. Conversely, we feel joyful and peaceful out of our "good treasure," by right of consciousness.

Our teaching offers that whatever appears wrong is not wrong in itself but is our wrong perception of what is right. The distress is not about that e-mail or any external stimuli. It is our reminder to look again for insight into what this has come to teach us. When we look again, this time through God's eyes, we open ourselves to see truth and experience it through love.

After my friend calmed down, she reread the e-mail and was surprised to find that it did not contain the upsetting message she originally perceived. She realized that the only problem was her attitude. She then responded to the e-mail—with *love*.

Ernest Holmes reminds us, "It is up to the individual to put negative feelings in their proper place, recognize them for what they really are, and proceed to affirm the nature of Spirit within. ... Approach a problem with eyes open and know that there is a solution."

As an act of faith, let's look again, choose to see through God's eyes, and recognize that there is nothing to fear and nothing against us. Looking through the eyes of God, we always perceive *love*.

—Published in the July 2012 Science of Mind *magazine*

# Fierce Grace Calls

*How precious did that grace appear the hour I first believed.*

— John Newton, "Amazing Grace"

Our families of origin seem to double as our laboratories and inner workshops. These relationships offer us the real-time opportunity for continuous self-realization. They coax us to stand for ourselves—for the truth of who we are—regardless of appearances or hearsay. We often misconstrue their tow. When we face challenging times or experience compelling conflict in familial and spousal relationships, we often find ourselves demanding of Infinite Intelligence: "Why me? What have I done to deserve this?" Fierce grace calls us to look deeply into the mirror and gracefully and adeptly untie ourselves from the past to discern how our lives came to be as they are now.

My friend and clairaudient, Paul Selig, encourages this awareness: "I know who am; I know what I am; I know how I serve." Standing in this knowing helps us realize and accept that all of our current relationships are simply an out-picturing of former beliefs. We *can* and *must* release ourselves from the consciousness of limitation that binds us to the past. First, we can accept this as an opportunity for a lesson well-learned; then, we can harness our inner resolve to know, affirm, and act as if "I love myself better than this, *and* I have the right and facility to change the trajectory of my life."

We must cease believing that our historical patterns wield power over us, renounce our so-called humanhood, and claim our divine selfhood. I know grace to be unmerited favor that lights my life from the inside out and helps me see that the Divine order and good includes me. Fierce grace thoroughly illuminates and empowers me to see clearly who I am and how I must truly *be* in this awareness in order to act with bold authenticity, in truth.

*"Twas grace that brought us safe thus far and grace will lead us home."*

—Published in the April 2013 Science of Mind *magazine*

# Honor the Holy

Earlier this year, a Florida jury acquitted George Zimmerman of second-degree murder charges in the shooting death of Trayvon Martin. This verdict, as in other high-profile criminal cases, rocked our collective consciousness and still today renders me in tears. Many of us judged, blamed, slandered, and ultimately withdrew from our typical level of ease with each other. Once again, we took sides and squared off in dueling punditry.

Having hunkered down on one side of the outcome or the other, we forgot that *all* life is precious and *everyone* is equally worthy of love, acceptance, and forgiveness. In one of our summer-school sessions, our beloved Forgiveness Masters reminded us to pray for Martin, Zimmerman, their families, and the jurors. They said, "Remember, anyone who has lost their way and whose behavior attests to the fact, if you're not praying for them, you are in collusion with them."

Allen Ginsberg writes, simply, "Holy! Holy! Holy! The world is holy! The soul is holy!" Yes, that's it! *Holy.* There are no people anywhere who have a belief system, skin color, sexual orientation, or behavior that renders them less than holy.

Now, that's a mouthful and a heartful. I acknowledge that I am often challenged to recognize or honor the holy in myself or others. Even though our awareness and belief in the indwelling God is the greatest single determinant in our lives, situations and circumstances dare us to recognize or even discern God within and around all of us. Although the world invites us to do an external search, this is truly an inward journey. There is nowhere to go, no thing to find, just the truth to be revealed from the inside out: We are holy.

Eddie Watkins Jr.'s revelation in the song, "All the Same Stuff," makes it plain and challenges our critical thinking:

> *If God is all there is, you see,*
> *What else could anything else be?*
> *It's all the same stuff*
> *You're free to rearrange it any way you want!*

Let's rearrange it so we recognize and honor the presence of God in all, at all times. After all, what else could anything be ... but holy?

—Published in the December 2013 Science of Mind *magazine*

# Choose this Day to See God in All

I am a huge fan of the movies *What the Bleep Do We Know?!* and *The Matrix*. Both films feature lead characters in personal/spiritual crisis, each experiencing a unique dark night of the soul. They yearn, like Bill Thetford, scribe for *A Course in Miracles* (ACIM), for "a better way." These protagonists are worth studying. Their journeys led them to seek, expand their consciousness, and ultimately find a better way.

This is no small feat.

In *Creative Mind*, Holmes writes, "To acquire the larger consciousness is no easy task. All that we have believed in which contradicts the perfect whole must be dropped from our thought. We must see that we are one in the great One."

These works also creatively portray our adeptness at downplaying living our true purpose and resisting change, even when we recognize that it will benefit us. All three—ACIM, *The Matrix*, and *What the Bleep*, along with many others—offer evidence of how we might realize the presence of God in all, the true nature of reality, clues for living life more fully and experiencing life in a better way.

Whenever we choose to live as full participants and honor spiritual principle, we live as the spiritual beings we truly are. Joshua 24:15 admonishes us to "… choose this day whom ye will serve; whether [it will be] the gods which your fathers served." Our "choosing" beckons us beyond our ingrained thinking pattern and our attachment to past ways. We are called to begin, in earnest, to choose righteously, live in the present, and work to continuously expand our capacity to recognize and ignite the highest and best in ourselves and others.

The key is to acknowledge that we are unbounded spiritual beings and live in accord with the divine creative flow, in nonresistance to a power greater than we are. As we begin to change and consistently serve a higher calling, a better way is revealed, and ultimately we can declare with Joshua: *"As for me and my house, we will serve the Lord."*

—Published in the June 2014 Science of Mind *magazine*

# Handle the Truth

*We've got the power to restore, refresh our life;
we've got the evidence that everything will be alright.*

— Brance McKenzie, "We Be the Majesty"

There is an infamous and inflammatory line during a court scene in the movie *A Few Good Men* in which Jack Nicholson's character, Col. Jessup, responding to Lt. Kaffee's demand, "I want the truth!," he shouts, "You can't handle the truth!"

Col. Jessup then spews his self-righteous, arrogant assumption that his sense of right is best for all. He essentially says that none of us really want to know what we have endorsed and must forfeit in order to maintain the status quo—our current systems and conditions exactly as they are. He believes we'd rather not be made aware of the specific orders required and how the enforcement of laws must be executed to ensure a system of what really is inequities.

In truth, the status quo ensures our world does not work for everyone. Instead, it works to keep some out and others down. What is most frightening about Col. Jessup's wickedly scripted testimony is that it mirrors our experience. While we are determined to seek the truth, too often we seem unwilling to handle the truth that on our watch, our elders and children are hungry and cold, or that women, People of Color, and same-gender-loving people are refused equal access.

What if we were willing to, as the Declaration of Independence states, "hold these truths to be self-evident, that all [humans] are created equal, that they are endowed by their Creator with certain unalienable Rights, that among these are Life, Liberty, and the pursuit of Happiness"?

To handle these truths, we would have to stand even more boldly committed and resolutely call forth a world that works for everyone. We would have to release our fear that our nation, tribe, and loved ones might not fare as well if we allowed our differences to be embraced and celebrated instead of feared.

This is the truth that sets us free. And in the end, we can handle the truth, knowing that we are the authors of our destiny, and we cannot change what we do not acknowledge.

—*Published in the July 2015* Science of Mind *magazine*

# Center Down

*Be still and know that I am God.*

— Psalm 46:10

In preparation for Black History Month, I recalled that Dr. Martin Luther King carried a copy of Dr. Howard Thurman's book, *Jesus and the Disinherited*, on his travels. It is said that this book, especially, informed King's consciousness and methodology. Thurman wrote of "… the striking similarity between the social position of Jesus in Palestine and that of the vast majority of American Negroes… ." He also wrote of the necessity of dodging the three hounds of hell, "fear, hypocrisy, and hatred," and the importance of embracing our "inward center" to do so.

Thurman's treatise, originally published in 1949, is as relevant today as it was when written. Today, there is increased evidence of systemic discriminatory practices and imposed limits based on ethnicity (also on gender and sexual orientation). The dream of racial equality and human equity has been painfully slow to manifest, and frequently the hounds of hell snap viciously at our heels.

Similarly, author Caroline Myss suggests, "[O]ne of the healthiest ways to counter the nonsense coming at us from the outside world … is to continue to build a strong and solid reservoir of wisdom and truth in your soul."

This is what Thurman called "knowing God as self." It is from this consciousness that we can begin embracing our inward center. This intention and practice works and translates to an essential survival technique for those oppressed.

When disaster strikes, even as we are doing our best to know God, and we are consumed by anguish, our faith shaken, we are in a state similar to the father in Mark 9:24, who wailed in despair, "Lord, I believe; help thou mine unbelief." It is then that we most need to be still, and follow Thurman, who wrote:

> *How good it is to center down! To sit quietly and see one's self pass by! The streets of our minds seethe with endless traffic. Our spirits resound with clashings, with noisy silences, while something deep within hungers and thirsts for the still moment and the resting lull.*

For now, let us *be* still and *know*.

—Published in the February 2016 Science of Mind magazine

## Practice Is Key

*The aim of evolution is to produce a man who, at the objective point of his own self-determination, may completely manifest the inner life of the Spirit.*

— Ernest Holmes

During a recent Golden State Warriors game, player Stephen Curry hit the most impressive game-winner ever. I watched in awe as he ran up the court and shot a record-breaking 38-foot jump shot with only 0.06 seconds left on the clock.

At the risk of exposing my severe Curry-mania, I make note that Curry succeeded in breaking his own NBA record for the most three-pointers made in a season, as well as becoming the first player in history to make at least ten three-pointers in back-to-back games. It's as if nothing can stop him.

In an interview, his teammate Klay Thompson acknowledged he is no longer surprised by Curry. "We've seen him practice from that range every day," Thompson said. Yes! Practice is key. This is consistent with what I have discerned about mastery. Speakers, teachers, singers, dancers, and spiritual practitioners—they practice. Malcolm Gladwell suggests that all mastery is preceded by a minimum of 10,000 hours of practice.

The truth is, only Steph Curry can stop Steph Curry. He could, like many of us do, begin taking his gift for granted and not work to improve it. He could recite self-deprecating affirmations, listen to and give credibility to haters, or let doubt erode his confidence. Instead, Curry describes his approach this way: "Every time I rise up, I have confidence that I am going to make it. I've never been afraid of big moments. I get butterflies. I get nervous and anxious, but I think those are all good signs that I'm ready for the moment."

For sure, living a powerful life requires preparation, and as Gladwell gauged, at least 10,000 hours of engagement (aka, practice). The 10,000 hours will, of necessity, include several muscle-building yet failed attempts.

Our challenge is to believe and know there is nothing in the Law opposing our success. Once we claim this certainty, our practice and engagement become the path to a powerful life.

For which "big moment" are you practicing?

—*Published in the June 2016* Science of Mind *magazine*

# January Reset

*Do not think that I have come to revoke the written Law or the Prophets;*
*I am not come to revoke but to fulfill.*

— Matthew 5:17

January is the perfect time to set and declare our highest intent for 2017 and to bless, honor, and make peace with the past. This month, we celebrate Dr. Martin Luther King Jr.'s birthday. Our national holiday, in celebration of his legacy, consistently inspires my reset each New Year. I marvel at King's courage in standing boldly in the face of systemic terror and lawlessness. As we launch 2017, we are empowered to simultaneously claim life anew. We are called to expand in greater self-awareness, selflessness, and authentic self-expression.

Last fall, the African American Museum opened in our nation's capital. It opened to long lines and critical acclaim. There was also venomous ridicule. There were many who celebrated this long-overdue telling of our story and this safe space for the history, artifacts, and future of African Americans. There were those who questioned the need for a museum focused on people of the African diaspora. The questions seem to dismiss the fact that this museum seeks to tell a story, at its best and worst, which has often been inaccurately portrayed or gone untold.

The museum also represents a new beginning, an opportunity to tell our collective history through an African-American lens. The intention is not to rewrite, compete with, or bring disrepute to any other museum of American history. Instead, the purpose is to—as the Nazarene is said to have clarified and King clearly actualized in his social justice work—not to revoke, but to fulfill. It is to fulfill the Divine Principle at the core of our Declaration of Principles: that all have rights, by Law, to "life, liberty and the pursuit of happiness."

I begin 2017 knowing, as Holmes suggested, "The starting point to creating a better future is to deliberately free our minds of the mistakes of yesterday and feel that they are no longer held against us; they no longer need to be a liability."

Inspired, I stand courageously for our highest and best—a world that works for everyone.

*—Published in the January 2017* Science of Mind *magazine*

# Pure Imagination

*If you want to view paradise, simply look around and view it.*
*Anything you want to, do it.*
*Wanna change the world? There's nothing to it.*
*There is no life I know to compare with pure imagination.*
*Living there, you'll be free, if you truly wish to be.*

—Willy Wonka, in the song "Pure Imagination"

The song "Pure Imagination" from the original *Willie Wonka and the Chocolate Factory* movie soundtrack is an oldie and goodie—one of my favorite tunes. I love the wisdom of harnessing our capacity to claim and experience freedom, first in mind, set to music.

Holmes put it this way: "Just imagine yourself surrounded by mind—so plastic, so receptive that it receives the slightest impression of your thought. Whatever you think, it takes up and executes for you. ... Whatever the pattern we provide, that will be our demonstration."

Since we tend to walk in the direction of—and draw into our experience—whatever we imagine, if we watch our thoughts, we get a pretty clear idea of what is going on within us.

Rather than doubting the veracity of our ability to call forth what we "truly wish to be," we can *know* and accept that our desire already exists as an option in the field of Infinite Possibility. What we desire is available, and we can choose it instead of any of the other possibilities magnetized by our feelings of inadequacy, doubt, and fear.

Each person is responsible for choosing.

This requires us to activate and engage the Creative Process through the virtual reality of our imagination. We do this when we focus our inner and outer vision—all that we sense, see, hear, and feel—to imagine what we desire as manifest. Holmes encourages us to engage our pure imagination, saying, "Imagine yourself to be what you want to be. See only that which you desire—refuse even to think of the other.

Stick to it, never doubt. Say many times a day, 'I am that thing'—realize what this means. It means that the great universal power of Mind is that, and It cannot fail."

What shall we imagine? Past disappointments and worst-case scenarios or a personal paradise and absolute freedom?

*—Published in the May 2017* Science of Mind *magazine*

# The Universe Awaits Your Order

*In principle and in potential, we are immersed in good for we are in the Mind of God. But we have freedom, or volition, to create in our own experience, out of the possibilities of life with which we have been endowed, the prerogative of heaven or hell.*

— Ernest Holmes

One of my favorite teaching metaphors uses a restaurant motif to illuminate how the universe awaits and fulfills our orders by right of consciousness. My fictional restaurant offers a full array of culinary options and experiences, as a metaphor for the bounty of life. Although there are far too many selections for any one person to order during one sitting, many diners choose not to venture past the dish they ordered last. Too often, this is their choice, even though the dish was not to their complete satisfaction.

As creatures of habit, we, too, suspend our right to choose and gravitate to the familiar, often at the expense of our highest and best. It is akin to staying in a job or relationship you abhor, afraid or unwilling to make a move. Like an eddy, we engage in circular thinking that binds us in a non-beneficial, repeating pattern.

Is this true in your life? How many opportunities might go undetected while you continue to choose what you've always chosen? Joshua 24:15 challenges us: "Choose you this day whom ye will serve; whether the gods which your fathers served..., or the gods of the Amorites..., but as for me and my house, we will serve the Lord."

It serves us to be attentive to the choices life offers us. Life can be good and very good, providing you with all that you long for and all you need. However, you are responsible for choosing and claiming the most desirable outcome for yourself. And you may have to grow through several possibilities, including various lesser choices and experiences, to manifest what you really want.

We must believe and know that the good we desire already exists and is available to us. All that we could possibly desire is awaiting our command and acceptance. Choose it!

Since the universe is awaiting our order, what will *you* choose?

—*Published in the July 2017* Science of Mind *magazine*

# Welcome! Please, Make Yourself at Home

*There is a significant difference between "all are welcomed here" and "this was created with you in mind."*

— Dr. Crystal Jones

During a recent exchange about making diversity and inclusion welcome in the workplace, I had an epiphany: Whatever any of us has, we had first to make it welcome. We had to create favorable conditions in mind and spirit for it and then provide sustenance for it to remain and continue to express in our lives. Whether we want it in our lives or detest it being there is irrelevant. What matters most is whether we create favorable conditions for it to flourish.

Sometimes we believe we are punished for our choices and behaviors. Not so. The sniffles and congestion you feel challenged by were welcomed by the ideal conditions for this disease, even though you did not intend your chronic lack of adequate rest plus insufficient nourishment to yield those results.

This undesirable manifestation is, however, a byproduct. The increase in your prosperity quotient is similarly a result of creating the necessary conditions, under which you demonstrate and experience greater prosperity. Manifesting your heart's desire requires being and doing something different, and this something must be in vibrational alignment with your desired outcome.

The same law applies in our personal lives and our world. The law is impersonal—an equal opportunity creator. Matthew 5:45 reminds us, "It rains on the just and unjust alike." When we think about creating welcoming environments and ecosystems of true inclusion, we know this intention requires more than putting out a welcome mat. It requires a welcoming spirit and an adaptation of how and what we have done to create the perfect conditions for the level of exclusion we currently have—something other than our desired outcomes.

Our heart's desire has a specific frequency and vibration. Our being and doing must match the frequency and vibration of our desire. As humans engaged in a spiritual life experience, and by right of consciousness, we are wholly free to create. As Paul Selig reminds us, "Nothing can be created without a conscious intention to bring it forth."

—*Published in the July 2019* Science of Mind *magazine*

# We're Here, So Let's Do This

Many are troubled by detailed reports that as of January 2019, the United States was separating thousands of migrant children from their families. We should find it untenable that authorities separated them without a reliable plan (possibly the intent?) to reunite them with their parents or guardians.

This crisis has been and will continue to be traumatic for the children, as it has been confirmed that many have been held without adequate food, bedding, soap, toothpaste, and clean clothing. Some allegedly have suffered mental, emotional, and physical mistreatment. All of this, tragically, on our watch.

I believe we, as Religious Scientists, are uniquely qualified to make a difference. Our mastery of affirmative treatment—knowing the truth and calling forth its highest expression—*and* our commitment to a world that works for everyone—standing for the highest and best for all concerned—empowers *all*. We can discern the truth and engage sufficient faith to see through the statistics and reports to a vision of a more humanitarian outcome.

Rather than give in to antagonism, I affirm the lyrics from "I'm Here," one of the songs on the soundtrack from the musical *The Color Purple*. This song always reminds me of the healing power of love and the essential nature of self-love in thriving. I am willing to stand in the gap and know this for all these children, declaring, as the song declares:

> *I believe I have inside of me*
> *Everything that I need to live a bountiful life.*
> *With all the love alive in me,*
> *I'll stand as tall as the tallest tree.*
> *And I'm thankful for every day that I'm given,*
> *both the easy and hard ones I'm livin'.*
> *But most of all, I'm thankful for lovin' who I really am. ...*
> *And I'm here!*

This declaration of "I'm here!" is empowering. It is reminiscent of Africans enslaved in the United States being referred to as the "people who refused to die."

The simple fact that these children *are* here and alive is a potent impetus. All children are *our* children, and nothing absolves us from taking responsibility for the well-being of *all* of our children. Through our prayers and our activism, we have direct access and a vested interest in declaring an outcome of safety, wholeness, and restoration.

We're here. Let's do this.

*—Published in the October 2019* Science of Mind *magazine*

# With Eyes Wide Open

*When we are not aware of God's goodness, grace, beauty, and unlimited wealth, we accept lack, restriction, and limitations as a part of life. The problem we experience has nothing to do with life; it is a function of our vision.*

— Iyanla Vanzant, *Acts of Faith*

In Luke 15:31, we find the parable of the prodigal son, an engaging story that represents our own lack of awareness and episodic schemes of separation. In this story, a son—representing each of us in our individual and collective consciousness—leaves the comfort and security of home for some worldly experience. He has fun for a while, begins living in violation of his family's cultural mores and values, and eventually devolves into suffering.

There is a turning point in which the son is said to have "come to himself," realizing that his suffering is optional. With this clarity, the prodigal son returns to the basics of knowing and honoring truth. He emerges, grounded in a willingness to do whatever is required to shift his experience. And in this, a solution is revealed.

He goes home. Going home is not easy for him and is not likely to be easy for us. Yet we suffer whenever we feel separate and engage in stories of separation. It is essential that we likewise return to a divine love relationship with self and the Living One.

Upon the prodigal son's return home, his father greets him with love and lavish generosity, saying to him, "My son, you are always with me, and everything that I have is yours." His father represents our guiding higher wisdom self that reminds us we already have—and have always had—all we need.

Our return "home" begins with our willingness to awaken and remain aware. We must remember to remember and practice trusting in the ever-present divine support and guidance.

As Iyanla Vanzant writes, "If we're going to move beyond the struggle, hardships, and restrictions we find in life, we must open our eyes and remember, 'All that the Father has is mine.'"

—Published in the January 2020 *Science of Mind* magazine

# Harriet Tubman

*If I'm free, my family should be, too. I made up my mind, I'm going back. …*
*I would give every last drop of blood in my veins*
*until this monster called slavery is dead!*

— Harriet Tubman

Since our 2009 inception, our center has embraced Harriet Tubman as our "Matron Saint." Last fall, when the film *Harriet* was released, we rented a cinema for a private viewing the opening weekend. Because Mother Harriet is such a powerful icon for us, we knew this was an essential film for our community to view together.

Most narratives offer a narrow sense of Mother Harriet: She escaped, made her way to freedom, and then returned to liberate others. This film breathed new life into old understandings and gave viewers the gift of Mother Harriet's humanity. We saw her engage the same universal principles on which we rely: love, perseverance, courage, faith, and trust. In our post-film dialogue and study guide, we focused on how she engaged and modeled these principles for us and how we might employ them in our current circumstances.

I particularly appreciated that the filmmaker focused on and depicted Mother Harriet's capacity for love and her commitment to freedom. In all the highlights and accounts of Mother Harriet's life, none had emphasized her love for her family and humanity as her motivation for her numerous return trips, at great personal risk, to free other enslaved people. Her objective always included helping others. Now we see her as a mirror image of our best intentions.

*Harriet* is a film for such a time as this and especially for our movement. It is not a movie about slavery. Instead, it illustrates the courage required of each of us to fulfill our commitment to freedom (in any of its manifestations).

*Harriet* filmmaker Kasi Lemmons said, "'To live free or die' is a very powerful concept. Tubman says over and over again. My favorite quote of hers is, 'I prayed to God to make me strong enough to fight.'"

That's fascinating for the time we live in. There's so much that we have to pray to be strong enough to fight for. For what or whom are we willing to fight?

—*Published in the February 2020* Science of Mind *magazine*

# A New Harvest

This is a time of immense change, and many of us are working to shift our experiences and outcomes, our sense of how we are to be and what we are to do. Some of us with African ancestry linked to American slavery are honoring the 156th anniversary of Juneteenth. While this celebration is a conundrum, it offers clarity as to the depth of systemic racism and illustrates how long Black lives have seemed to not matter. Even as we acknowledge centuries of violence-enforced segregation, we—in faith, believing—now launch our 2021 midyear resolutions.

We are reweaving the quilt of our lives into a higher vision. Life is for realizing our purpose and actualizing our divine contribution to the universe. There is a calling on each of our lives. Now is the perfect time to reassess, recalibrate, and reimagine our calling and live out our greatest yet to be.

The universe compels us to be our authentic selves. Our initial awareness may resonate as an inner urge. It often begins with the proverbial whisper, and depending on our attentiveness and responsiveness, this whisper may steadily increase to an attention-getting whack upside the head, providing a major and necessary blow to the status quo. Ouch!

Many of us can offer personal testimony to this experience and how often we have relied on pain to move us. Our reliance on pain as our motivation continues until we surrender this mental state and, in faith, allow our vision to magnetize our awaiting good. Each of us has a vital role in our every manifestation.

In the parable of the sower, the master teacher, Yeshua, instills that there is more required of us than spouting good thoughts, positive visions, and affirmations. We must ensure our thoughts and prayers are sown in a consciousness with the mental equivalent of our desired outcomes.

As we acknowledge Juneteenth 2021, let us do so with the intention of setting a new and healing cause in motion. Holmes reminds us, "There can be no new harvest without a new seedtime." Our seedtime or attitude is cause for every harvest.

If we truly desire different outcomes, we must first provide a new seedtime—an updated mental equivalent and commitment to a world that works for all.

—Published in the June 2021 *Science of Mind* magazine

# Speak to My Heart, Lord

*Speak to my heart, Lord, give me Your holy word.*
*If I can hear from You, then I'll know what to do.*
*I won't go alone, Lord, I'll never go on my own.*
*Just let Your spirit guide and let Your word abide.*

— Donnie McClurkin, "Speak to My Heart"

Countless times during this past year, I engaged these lyrics to soothe my soul. I would sing my own version: "Let Your spirit guide and let Your love abide. Speak to my heart, Lord." My spiritual practice and this song—these lyrics—helped me get through our current pandemics.

My experience of the past year helped me recognize just how much of what I thought I knew I did not actually know. However, what I know and trust for certain is that it works for me to stop, get still, tap in, and be receptive to Divine Spirit. To paraphrase Ralph Waldo Emerson, I get my bloated nothingness out of the way of the Divine and let It work through me.

Working through me is the only way It can work for and as me. This awareness is essential in calling forth a new normal. I acknowledge that much about the ways we have been with each other never really felt normal to me.

It took a pandemic and a racial reckoning for many to concede that we had normalized inhumane practices and policies. I know our experiences always manifest from a mental equivalent, so I pray our new normal more accurately reflects our highest intent and vision.

As we consistently hone our spiritual practices of meditation and prayer, we foster a keen listening for Spirit, divert our attention from fear and outer conditions, and tune in to divine guidance. This deepens our capacity to be still, silent, and open to Spirit. As McClurkin's song says:

*Message of love to encourage me.*
*Lifting my heart from the snare.*
*How You love me and care for me.*
*Speak to my heart.*

I pray that we, too, accept Spirit's guidance with expectancy and surrender to the wisdom and grace of Source, allowing divine inspiration to elevate our lives.

—*Published in the August 2021* Science of Mind *magazine*

## Let's Jump

*We have within us a power that is greater than anything we shall ever contact in the outer, a power that can overcome every obstacle in your life and set us safe, satisfied, and at peace, healed and prosperous, in a new light and in a new life.*

— Ernest Holmes

Holmes reminds us of the innate power we all have within us. My brother-teacher, Rev. Dr. Will Coleman, says, "We often think of spiritual height as an out-of-body experience. This is not the case. Spiritual height is embedded in the depths of our body. The higher you want to go up, the deeper you should go into the richness of your own being."

Going higher requires rooting deeper. Operating a pogo stick is a useful metaphor for this intention. Many of us recall jumping on a pogo stick or watching someone master the pogo jump. I recently gleaned the inner workings of the pogo stick.

Beyond getting both feet to stay on the pedals while applying downward pressure on the innerspring, I learned how the compressed spring releases energy and propels the pogo stick up. First, we must literally plunge down to jump up. Also, a portion of the energy remains within the spring after the first jump, so each subsequent jump adds energy and propels the jumper ever higher.

I get it. To fully rise up, we must first be grounded, rooted in Spirit. This is how we are wired. Everything we experience serves to energize our internal compression spring. Our next jump is divinely guided and supported so we can spring to even greater heights.

Think of this pogo stick to remember how going deep supports you in rising above obstacles. We already have within us everything required. Let's anchor ourselves in the mental equivalent and consciousness of our highest spiritual height—our intended outcome and greatest yet to be.

Our divine good will always manifest in perfect alignment with the height of our belief and the depth of our faith. Come on: Let's get jumping!

—Published in the September 2021 *Science of Mind* magazine

# Madiba: Imprisoned Splendor

*We cannot believe that our inner wholeness was created by us or came into being through a process of evolution. Quite the reverse. All evolution is a result of the action of an imprisoned splendor that exists at the center of all things.*

— Ernest Holmes

This Holmes quote immediately brought to mind Nelson Mandela, also known as Madiba. The trajectory of Mandela's life personifies imprisoned splendor. Mandela was a South African antiapartheid revolutionary, fugitive, political leader, and prisoner before he led his country from the tyranny of apartheid minority rule to a multicultural democracy. Jailed for twenty-seven years for his anti-apartheid activities and released in 1990, he became the first Black president and head of state of South Africa in 1994.

What manner of man was Mandela? Even while behind bars, imprisoned splendor was apparent. Mandela recounts reading and reciting William Ernest Henley's "Invictus" to his fellow prisoners. He was particularly inspired by the lines, "I am the master of my fate. I am the captain of my soul." This supported Mandela's inner healing and liberation. His written and spoken testimonies make clear that Mandela was set free long before the South African government released him from prison. His personal and political freedom came from the inside out.

Once released, he led the new government in dismantling apartheid, advanced his vision of racial reconciliation, and delivered a new constitution. Essential to his progress was establishing the Truth and Reconciliation Commission to investigate past human rights abuses.

Mandela's consciousness and actions earned him a Nobel Peace Prize in 1993 and the U.S. Presidential Medal of Freedom in 2002.

Morgan Freeman, who portrayed Mandela in the movie *Invictus*, said, "In bringing down the evil of apartheid, Mandela raised us up. His wisdom, patience, compassion, and insistence on reconciliation make us aspire to be better people. In his determination to break from the chains of the past, he allowed us all to join him as the masters of our fate and the captains of our souls."

—*Published in the February 2022* Science of Mind *magazine*

# A Lesson in Love

*Under His teaching, every relationship becomes a lesson in love.*

— *A Course in Miracles* (ACIM)

Many of us have experienced the trauma of the crash and burn of a close relationship. My mastermind group recently took a deep dive into how we perceive and express in our relationships—the doubts, fears, and judgments we hold. We acknowledged that, to a person, we have tripped, fallen, assumed a fetal position, and sometimes did not rise for a long while. We abdicated our spiritual practices, made some relationships special, and declared ourselves justified in our judgments. Stuck in a bleak sense of our circumstances, we focused on being right instead of seeking healing and reconciliation, instead of welcoming happiness.

We acknowledged that if we continued to perceive our relationships through an adversarial filter and lean toward separation, then oneness and connection would continue to evade us. We also owned our collective frustration, resistance, and reluctance to love ourselves and forgive our past behavior. Acquiescing to separation left us unhappy and suffering. Someone declared, "There has to be another way!" We all agreed and immediately invoked *A Course in Miracles* (ACIM).

We began studying ACIM together. That step helped us be aware of and shift our circular thinking, up leveling our thinking from fear to faith. We are releasing the past and staying attentive to the present, and our circumstances are morphing. We are beginning to see our relationships and our lives differently.

This shared experience is a huge blessing to me. I am more open to seeing Divine Spirit in and as me. I assign new meaning to challenging relationships and my past experiences. I gain clarity about how I get triggered, how to harness that energy, and how to own my emotions.

I truly am grateful for the safety of our mastermind group because it helped me reveal and acknowledge that the wounds I thought were healed—and the work I thought I finished—were not yet complete. Our relationship upsets provide the perfect motivation for all of us to shift, pivot, and heal. I am willing to embrace all of this as a lesson in love and call forth healing.

—*Published in the July 2022* Science of Mind *magazine*

# Passion and Purpose Aligned

*If you believe in your divine destiny, nothing else matters.*
*Your conquering, positive desire will overcome all seeming obstacles.*
*Your life will be molded according to your belief and vision. Not a hair*
*on your head will be harmed until your life mission has been fulfilled.*

— A.K. Mozumdar

I believe some people have always known their purpose in life. Even if their life journey looks circuitous, their stops and starts still cannot conceal the certainty of their purpose. It is visible in the fabric of their lives. The rest of us must be more intentional and invest in discerning our lives' purpose.

I found leadership coach Kevin Cashman's three Gs helpful in realizing a purpose-driven life. He inquires about the *g*ifts that energize us, what we desire to *g*ive, and what we need to *g*row. Our answers reveal how Spirit can more fully manifest Itself as our life purpose and divine destiny.

This is always an inside job. Passion is the fire within us, igniting our desires and fueling our purpose. Our purpose is as fluid as our inner calling and guiding light. Purpose is lived from the inside out. Focusing our passion to engage our purpose is key. To direct our passion toward our purpose, we must also trust. Know that, as Mozumdar taught, our lives always are being formed in the alignment of our belief and vision, our passion and purpose. When our passion and purpose align, we are grounded in the power of love. We manifest accordingly and with ease and grace.

Uncovering my purpose continues to be a journey of self-exploration. It requires focused self-awareness, introspection, and that I examine what sets my heart afire, what I am most passionate about. Ultimately, it requires that I align my passion with my purpose and commit to living it fully.

I am committed to living my life purpose from my passion. I know my life is formed and transformed according to my belief and vision. I sense how my passion informs and fuels my purpose. As I intertwine my passion and purpose, I grow in courage and faith that overcomes all challenges to living my life purpose. In this way, I am empowered to ride my inspiration and enthusiasm from possibility and potential to joy and fulfillment.

—*Published in the August 2023* Science of Mind *magazine*

# *Divine Paradox*

*There's a perfect shot out there trying to find each and every one of us. What we got to do is get ourselves out of its way; let it choose us.*

— Will Smith, in The Legend of Bagger Vance

This is one of my favorite quotes from one of my favorite movies. Will Smith plays the title role of a charismatic spiritual guide and the soul of the film. This film is about grace, redemption, and the opportunity and willingness to make a fresh start.

It employs golf as a metaphor for how we play the game of life and centers around a golfer's struggle to overcome hardship and his inner demons. Matt Damon plays the golfer. Like me, he must learn to let go of the burdens of the past and future and center his focus on the present moment and journey. His mystical caddy, Bagger Vance, aids him in regaining his confidence and standing during a major competition. The goal: Eliminate struggle, get back in the swing, and win. Vance coaches the golfer to be in harmony with his golf clubs, and this simultaneously supports him in harmonizing with his life. In this way, he regains his authentic swing.

It is paradoxical. The paradox lies in concurrently engaging surrender and self-mastery. This is my challenge. The golfer is torn between his desire to control the efficacy of his swing and adhering to Vance's guidance to surrender to the flow of the game. The golfer's frustration depicted in the film is also mine in life, balancing two seemingly opposing forces—surrender and action.

The film captures the essence of the spiritual principle, "It is done unto you as you believe," and reminds me that true mastery comes not from forceful control, but from balancing surrender and self-mastery. It choreographs a dance of acting and trusting the process. It also elucidates the paradoxical nature of achieving success and fulfillment in life through surrender.

In time, instead of giving in to the pressures of living and struggling against the divine flow of life, our golfer ultimately surrenders and allows both his golf stroke and his life to be divinely guided. This is my lesson, and I get more out of my way and into the divine flow of life with every viewing.

—Published in the October 2023 Science of Mind *magazine*

## *Wilt Thou Be Made Whole?*

*When Jesus saw him lying there, and knew that he already had been in that condition a long time, He said to him, "Wilt thou be made whole?"*

— John 5:6

Many of us have written and lived horror stories, even worse than that man by the pool, referenced above, under our own production and direction. We do our own stunts, design special effects, and underwrite CGI, all at great personal expense. Fully committed, we create powerful dramas replete with all the makings of a blockbuster. We script and perform the requisite scenes of anguish, shame, betrayal, guilt, and regret. The plot builds until the camera finds us standing alone in front of the dreaded door—the grotesque heavy wood or stone door featured in the pivotal scene in old horror movies.

We are there now, and the audience gets involved: "Nooo! Run! Don't go through that door!" Why does the audience shout for us to stop? As our inner witnesses, they watched us construct our way to the door, so they know a dreadful experience awaits us behind it.

How did we end up in front of that dreaded door? We consistently believed and behaved in accordance with our disempowering beliefs. There was a specific and unique combination of thoughts, beliefs, and behaviors required to get us here, and we repeatedly embraced these.

What happens next is up to you. Will you be made whole, choosing to honor your divinity? Or will you cross the threshold and delve deeper into your horror experience?

In his book, *Handle With Prayer*, Alan Cohen says that to think is to create. "The notion of something coming into existence without a thought preceding it is as preposterous as a flower growing without a seed to start it."

As you pause before the door, consider this: Believing X got you here; and continuing to believe X will keep you here. Only when you believe and embrace more empowering thoughts will you manifest more empowering results. Remember, all thoughts create according to their own kind. What thoughts will you choose today?

—Published in the December 2023 Science of Mind *magazine*

## SECTION 8

# Vision, Voice, and Action

## FROM THE INSIDE OUT

*The proof that one truly believes is in action.*

— Bayard Rustin

## Step Up and Out in Faith

*We must address the collective unconsciousness that perpetuates the ideas of separation. We do this by expanding our awareness and understanding that we swim in the embodiment of White privilege and systemic racism and that we are all subject to this trauma being passed down through generations. The radical understanding of oneness calls us to address these issues.*

— Rev. Sunday Cote

When Hank Aaron died earlier this year, I was reminded of our collective pride when he became baseball's new Home Run King in 1974. He tied Babe Ruth's record of 714 on April 4, 1974, and broke the record on April 8.

He was immediately inundated with hate mail from people who did not want to see a Black man break Ruth's record. The U.S. Postal Service recorded that he received some 3,000 letters a day during this period. Aaron and his family required professional security because of the death threats they received.

We want the centuries of oppression and terror to be behind us, yet the consciousness remains. Even today, we see a continual pattern of discrimination, terror, and trauma.

It seems the very existence of same-gender loving persons or those who look, sound, or believe differently is of tremendous offense to some group and engenders various forms of mental, emotional, and physical violence. When will we truly embrace oneness and the radical practice of inclusion?

Inclusion requires a bold shift. There is no way to transform our environment without first changing our minds. Our consistent thoughts create our current conditions. In "These Boots Were Made for Walking," Nancy Sinatra sang, "You keep samin' when you ought to be a-changin'." Come on folks, we gotta change. No more behaving the same as we have and expecting different outcomes.

We know thought is the true causative force, and whatever we hold in mind and heart becomes imprinted and out-pictured in our environment. It's time to transform our thinking and accept each other. Let's step up and out in faith and fully embrace oneness.

—*Published in the April 2021* Science of Mind *magazine*

# New Money Showing the Way

*Question: How are we to treat others? Answer: There are no others.*

— Ramana Maharshi

We have come a long way as a nation. Although much has changed, we still have work to do in expanding our sense of oneness, our national capacity for acceptance, and our standards for inclusion.

In April 2016, the Treasury Department announced that Harriet Tubman, a formerly enslaved person who escaped to freedom and returned to free others, would be on the front of the $20 bill, moving U.S. President Andrew Jackson to the back.

Treasury Secretary Jacob J. Lew said that in the public comments regarding the choice of Mother Harriet, "The pattern became clear that Harriet Tubman struck a chord with people in all parts of the country, of all ages."

Mother Harriet's life while enslaved, as an abolitionist and conductor on the Underground Railroad, as a Civil War soldier, nurse, spy, and scout, and as a social reformer and charitable citizen are all important facets of her humanity and her lifelong service and dedication to freedom. The Cherokee Nation also applauded this change, noting Tubman's "legacy represents values everyone can be proud of."

Indeed. For many People of Color, Harriet Tubman has near patron saint status. I think about all the Americans who have never seen an image similar to their own on our U.S. currency. My ancestors would surely shout and celebrate this change to include one they held in high esteem. I can hardly fathom the positive impact on our youth, holding a virtual history lesson in their hands every time they circulate a $20 bill.

Change is definitely afoot: There will be other women on our paper money as well. The U.S. Treasury is adding images of Sojourner Truth, Lucretia Mott, Susan B. Anthony, Alice Paul, and Elizabeth Cady Stanton to the back of the new $10 bill. Also, Eleanor Roosevelt, Rev. Dr. Martin Luther King Jr., and Marian Anderson will be depicted on the back of the new $5 bill. Be still my soul!

These welcome changes to expand our circle remind me of Ernest Holmes's words: "We cannot only embrace ourselves; somehow our arms must find themselves around the shoulders of all humanity."

Our new money may actually help some of us to realize and embrace that there really are no others.

*Note: The changes to U.S. currency described in this entry were approved under the administration of U.S. President Barack Obama but were not implemented by the following administration.*

—Published in the August 2016 Science of Mind *magazine*

# A Change Gon' Come

*It's been a long, a long time coming.*
*But I know a change gon' come, oh yes it will.*

— Sam Cooke, "A Change Is Gonna Come"

Alicia Garza inspired a powerful movement when she reminded us that Black Lives Matter. In anticipation of George Zimmerman's acquittal, after he killed Trayvon Martin, she founded #BlackLivesMatter to bring to light how consistently undervalued Black lives are in America. This international effort is transforming the Black Civil Rights Movement. She says, "Too bad we have to say it, but it's bringing people together."

Thank goodness we are coming together and that #BlackLivesMatter is energizing much needed change. Of course, there are those who take exception and assert, "All lives matter!" I agree, all lives do matter.

However, this response misses the point. The real issue is the combined effect of centuries of ingrained systemic prejudice, racism, and legalized brutality that give the consistent impression, backed by actions, that Black lives do not matter.

If indeed, all lives matter, our systems would be designed to ensure that all lives—all humans—are treated with reverence and respect and are held to the same lawful standard.

Black Lives Matter is a prophetic pronouncement on par with words spoken by the formerly enslaved Sojourner Truth in 1851 at the Women's Rights Convention in Akron, Ohio. In this legendary speech, she brilliantly argues that the platform for women's rights must include Black women. She was asking, "Aren't we the same?" Or as we find in Malachi 2:10, "Have we not all one Father? Hath not one God created us?"

#BlackLivesMatters is the equivalent of standing in similar powerful form, as a bold and earnest gesture, calling out in strong and truthful tones for human equity now.

In 1851, it might have been posed as "Ain't we human? Don't Black Lives Matter, too?" The humane response, then and now, being, "Of course, Black Lives Matter. We are one!" How can we work together to ensure this is evident?

In a consciousness of oneness, Sam Cooke sings for all of us:
> *There been times that I thought I couldn't last for long.*
> *But now I think I'm able to carry on.*
> *It's been a long, a long time coming.*
> *But I know a change gon' come, oh yes it will.*

—*Published in the December 2015* Science of Mind *magazine*

# Remembering the Greatest Souls

*And when great souls die,*
*after a period peace blooms,*
*slowly and always*
*irregularly. ...*
*They existed. They existed.*
*We can be.*
*Be and be better. For they existed.*

—Dr. Maya Angelou, "When Great Trees Fall"

Just ten days before Dr. Maya Angelou passed last May [2014], I was on a conference call where she was a presenter. Since her passing, I read her works with new meaning.

The poem referenced above, written and read in remembrance of James Baldwin, reveals her grace and exposes her generous spirit and incredible capacity for unabashedly including and honoring others.

Angelou's words summon us to acknowledge how we have been touched and restored in our remembrance of great souls. Her poem is prophetic in that many of us now feel that we can "be and be better" because she existed.

Angelou did not just exist, she thrived. She was larger than life.

She achieved a measure of success in everything she did: writing, dancing, singing, acting, teaching, speaking, mentoring, and cooking. She lived her life as a mother, daughter, sister, aunt, friend, and true Renaissance woman.

Over six decades, her bright light, wit, and accessibility captured our attention. Her wisdom, weighted like an anchor of conviction, transformed our doubt and expanded our hearts.

In the late 1980s, I read an interview with Angelou that cracked open my heart. She said, "You are the only person who can forgive you. Once that forgiving has taken place, you can then console yourself with the knowledge that a diamond is the result of extreme pressure. ... The pressure can make you into something quite precious, quite wonderful, quite beautiful, and extremely hard."

No matter how we choose to remember her, Angelou made her peace long ago and expressed it brilliantly:

> *You may write me down in history*
> *With your bitter, twisted lies,*
> *You may trod me in the very dirt.*
> *But still, like dust, I'll rise.*

—Published in the January 2015 Science of Mind *magazine*

# The Strategist and Tactician

*The soul that is within me no man can degrade.*

— Frederick Douglass

Leaders of six prominent Civil Rights groups joined forces in organizing the 1963 March on Washington: A. Phillip Randolph, Brotherhood of Sleeping Car Porters; Roy Wilkins, NAACP; Dr. Martin Luther King Jr., Southern Christian Leadership Conference (SCLC); James Farmer, Congress of Racial Equality; John Lewis, Student Nonviolent Coordinating Committee; and Whitney Young, National Urban League.

The organizations they represented proffered that economic issues and racial justice are inextricably intertwined.

In their wisdom, organizers included Bayard Rustin as the strategist and tactician. A master organizer, political intellectual, and pacifist, Rustin in 1947 created and rode in the first Freedom Rides, challenging segregation on interstate buses. Along with King, Rustin was one of the founders of the SCLC.

As an openly gay man during a time of fear and intolerance, Rustin was directed to work largely in the background. His skill, moral courage, and commitment to nonviolence made him enormously valuable and influential. The success of the march is attributed to him. At its close, Rustin confidently took the mic and read the demands the Civil Rights leaders would take to President John F. Kennedy.

A lifelong activist, Rustin stood boldly for peace and equal rights, demonstrating, organizing, and protesting around the world.

He died in 1987 at age seventy-five. In 2013, President Barak Obama posthumously awarded him the Presidential Medal of Freedom, saying, "Fifty years after the March on Washington he organized, America honors Bayard Rustin as one of its greatest architects for social change and a fearless advocate for its most vulnerable citizens."

—Published as the Daily Guide for February 22, 2024,
Science of Mind *magazine*

## THE ARCHITECT

*In a democracy, every citizen, regardless of his interest in politics, "holds office;" every one of us is in a position of responsibility; and, in the final analysis, the kind of government we get depends upon how we fulfill those responsibilities.*

— U.S. President John F. Kennedy, *Profiles in Courage*

In honor of the sixtieth anniversary of the March on Washington, I recognize and acknowledge A. Philip Randolph, founder and president of the Brotherhood of Sleeping Car Porters union and AFL-CIO executive, for his role as the march architect and his long-term commitment and contribution to the Civil Rights Movement.

In the 1900s, the Pullman Company was the largest employer of African Americans. In 1925, Randolph created the Brotherhood of Sleeping Car Porters. I recall the deep admiration our community held for Pullman porters. Although many were college graduates and respected in their communities, they were still paid low wages and subjected to disrespect and discriminatory practices. In the ten years Randolph led the union, porters realized increased wages, a shorter work week, and overtime pay.

He served as president of the National Negro Congress, an organization created to pressure U.S. President Franklin Delano Roosevelt to institute policies designed to treat African Americans fairly in the workplace and to protect their civil rights.

He initiated the 1941 March on Washington Movement, calling for thousands of Black people to assemble at the Lincoln Memorial in Washington, D.C., on July 1, 1941, to demand the president act. When Randolph refused to call off the march, Roosevelt responded by issuing an executive order forbidding "discrimination in the employment of workers in defense industries or government because of race, creed, color, or national origin."

Randolph collaborated with other Black leaders on the 1963 March, calling for freedom and prodding the pending Civil Rights bill into law.

*—Published as the Daily Guide for February 21, 2024, Science of Mind magazine*

# The Heart of the Question

*Racism is so universal in this country, so widespread and deep-seated, that it is invisible because it is so normal.*

— Shirley Chisholm, *Unbought and Unbossed*

It is certain that in the exact moment a baby takes its first breath, someone, somewhere is simultaneously releasing their final breath. In a similar fashion, I have taken the liberty of connecting two major historical events that took place on June 11, 1963, the first in Washington, D.C., the second in Jackson, Mississippi.

That year was a key time in the Civil Rights Movement, and President Kennedy was focused on the ever-increasing number and size of demonstrations, and the violent backlash from White supremacists and segregationists. We saw photos of Black children attacked by dogs and blasted with high-pressure firehoses.

When Governor George Wallace blocked the doorway of the University of Alabama to prevent two Black students' entry, Kennedy knew Civil Rights legislation was necessary. He decided to speak to the nation about this.

"The heart of the question," he said, "is whether all Americans are to be afforded equal rights and equal opportunities, whether we are going to treat our fellow Americans as we want to be treated. If an American, because his skin is dark, cannot eat lunch in a restaurant open to the public, if he cannot send his children to the best public school available, if he cannot vote for the public officials who will represent him, if, in short, he cannot enjoy the full and free life which all of us want, then who among us would be content to have the color of his skin changed and stand in his place? Who among us would then be content with the counsels of patience and delay?"

The next morning, the news reported the assassination of Medgar Evers.

—Published as the Daily Guide for February 18, 2024,
Science of Mind *magazine*

# Jim Crow Must Go

*Let me appeal to the consciences of many silent, responsible citizens of the White community who know that a victory for democracy in Jackson will be a victory for democracy everywhere.*

— Medgar Evers

Medgar Evers was the first field secretary for the NAACP in Mississippi. He demonstrated. He organized voter registration drives and boycotts. He investigated murders throughout the state for nine years and heroically worked to find justice for Emmet Till. He doggedly helped integrate the University of Mississippi, "Old Miss," supporting James Meredith in successfully registering and being admitted.

Although his work was met with hostility and made him a target of White segregationists, he never lost faith.

Evers, feeling overjoyed by President Kennedy's speech, on June 11, 1963, arrived home shortly after midnight, carrying T-shirts that said, "Jim Crow Must Go." He was shot in the back as he exited his car. Evers's wife and three children, still awake after watching President Kennedy's speech, heard the shot, quickly came outside, and found him lying in a pool of blood. His eyes met hers and he bravely asked her to, "Sit me up, turn me loose." Evers died within the hour.

I imagine that Evers planned to participate in the iconic March on Washington on August 28, 1963. There, thousands of demonstrators of many ethnicities marched and celebrated the proposed Civil Rights bill and mourned the death of Evers, a Civil Rights hero. It would take thirty-one years to convict his assassin.

President Kennedy was assassinated just three months later. The reforms he envisioned and shared that fateful night would become the Civil Rights Act of 1964, the most comprehensive social justice legislation to date. Although Kennedy and Evers never met, their aims and visions are forever intertwined in history.

—*Published as the Daily Guide for February 19, 2024,*
Science of Mind *magazine*

# Whitewashing History

*Whose children are we talking about? Black parents talk to their kids about racism. Asian American parents talk to their kids about racism. Just say that you don't want White kids to learn about racism.*

— LaGarrett King

U.S. President Joe Biden said, "Acknowledging some dark periods in our past is important," alluding to efforts to sanitize American history.

Case in point: The Florida Board of Education approved new standards for African American history, and it seems high school students will be taught a distorted and whitewashed history of the Ocoee massacre of 1920. A more accurate telling of this tragedy reveals that Whites attacked and killed Black residents of Ocoee, Florida, when two Black men attempted to vote.

It was not true, as was reported at the time, that "acts of violence were first perpetrated by African Americans." Dozens of Black residents were killed in the ultimate act of voter suppression, the rest forced to flee and their property seized. This is not accurately reflected in many history books.

In his address, President Biden said, "At a time when some seek to ban books and bury history, we're making it clear that we can't just choose to learn only what we want to know. We should learn everything that's good, bad, and the truth about who we are as a nation. That's what good nations do, and we are the greatest of all nations. Only with truth comes healing and justice and another step toward forming a more perfect union."

Only by telling the whole truth is reconciliation possible. Just as the truth was withheld and whitewashed to conceal what happened in Ocoee, the current legislation strives to do the same thing by conflating historical facts with contrived revisionist narratives. Now is our opportunity to declare the truth and commence healing and reconciliation.

*—Published as the Daily Guide for February 15, 2024,*
*Science of Mind magazine*

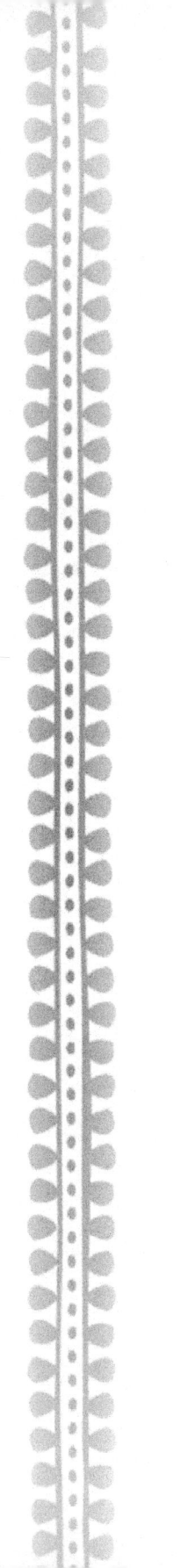

## SECTION 9

# Allies, Advocates, and Co-conspirators

## FROM THE INSIDE OUT

*We must take sides. Neutrality helps the oppressor, never the victim.
Silence encourages the tormentor, never the tormented.*

— Elie Wiesel

# Changing the Status Quo

*We all have a responsibility to create a just society.*

— Bryan Stevenson

I often hear folks I wish would behave as allies and advocates engage in discourse around not being responsible for slavery, Black Codes, Jim Crow, and separate and unequal housing, schools, and policing. It is obvious to me that while so many benefited for generations from these and other inequities, far fewer see themselves stepping forward to acknowledge and take responsibility and accountability for current inequities.

When we study our common history, we may not perceive ourselves to be responsible for slavery and systemic oppression. However, we are all accountable for setting right the truth of our past and working to create a just and fair future.

This is a call out to everyone in divine discomfort, everyone with a heart for freedom, justice, and equality. There is a higher calling for us to be and do from an intention of freedom, peace, justice, and equality for all.

This is also about change, about changing how we are and how we deepen our listening and act in alignment with what we say we believe. This call to action is to not just hear each other but to listen and respond with understanding, acceptance, support, and love.

Sometimes change occurs through individual advocacy, through policy reform, through protests, boycotts, or lawsuits. Sometimes a photo speaks a thousand words. Remember the iconic photo of a young man blocking a line of military tanks at Beijing's Tiananmen Square on June 5, 1989? He and that photo remain powerful symbols of courage and defiance.

If our intention is to change the status quo, we need more allies, advocates, and co-conspirators to demonstrate commitment, clarity, and courage in defying our current oppressive models.

*—Published as the Daily Guide for February 8, 2024,*
Science of Mind *magazine*

# Many Feelings About Segregation

*The organizers and perpetrators of segregation are as much the enemy of America as any foreign invader.*

— Bayard Rustin

Drew Gilpin Faust, the first female president of Harvard University, demonstrates the qualities of an advocate. She seems to have been born with a spirit for necessary trouble. She said she was raised to embrace the revisionist "glorious triumphs" of Confederacy myths.

In 1954, the Brown v. Board of Education Supreme Court decision challenged racial segregation, and integration was to become the law of the land with "all deliberate speed." However, by 1957, multiple states challenged the decision, including Virginia, Faust's home state. She knew, even then, she needed to act. She wrote to President Eisenhower, urging him to integrate schools. "Dear Mr. Eisenhower," her letter began. "I am nine years old, and I am White, but I have many feelings about segregation."

As Faust's advocacy evolved, she became a Civil Rights activist and historian of the cultural incongruence that shaped her youth. As a lifetime ally, she created a legacy of advocacy for the greater good, finding historical truth being distorted "preposterous and extremely distressing." Although raised on myths of faithful servants and benevolent masters, as a historian, she was unafraid to tell the story of a South Carolina planter who recorded his own oppressive and cruel slave mastery.

She communicates a certain clarity about the importance of ensuring truth and accuracy in our recorded history and truth in education. She challenges the notion that our children should not be uncomfortable with our past. "History," she says, "should make us uncomfortable."

She calls us into an awareness that truth is key to our healing and necessary trouble an antidote to the current dishonest discourse on Black history.

—Published as the Daily Guide for February 9, 2024,
Science of Mind *magazine*

# Someone Had To

*When my friend was assassinated for being nothing more than a Black man,
I decided it was time for that thing to be off the Statehouse grounds.
It's not just a symbol of hate; it's actually a symbol of pride in one's hatred.*

— South Carolina State Rep. Doug Brannon

On June 17, 2015, a mass shooting, now known as the Charleston Church Massacre, was perpetrated at the oldest Black church in the southern United States—the Emanuel African Methodist Episcopal Church. The nine people murdered were all African Americans, participating in the church's Bible study at the time of their deaths.

In the aftermath of this hate crime, concern and debate about, among other critical issues, the display and commemoration of the confederate flag at the South Carolina State House was elevated to national discourse.

Remember Bree Newsome, who climbed a flagpole at the South Carolina Capitol to remove that Confederate flag on June 27, 2015?

Newsome had many allies on her way to that flagpole and on the day she demonstrated such immense courage. Allies taught her how to climb the flagpole. Advocates arrived with bail money when she was arrested. Known and unknown co-conspirators were in the crowd.

As the police arrived to arrest Newsome, they approached the flagpole with tasers. Seeing this situation about to unfold, a White man placed his hand on the flagpole and stared into the eyes of the White police officers. This man knew that his privilege would interrupt the plan and keep Newsome safe. In that moment, this unknown man was a co-conspirator.

Action is the difference between an ally and advocate. Assuming personal risk is the mark of a co-conspirator. This inspires me to update "When you see something, say something" to "When you know something, do something." Our superpower is our knowing. We believe and know that all people are incarnations of the One Spirit—and each of us has an essential role to play in calling forth the greater good and a world that works for all.

Newsome unhooked the flag from the pole and passed it to a White man, James Tyson. When she made it down to the ground, police officers arrested them. She recited Psalm 23 as they were taken to jail.

*—Published as the Daily Guide for February 10, 2024,*
Science of Mind *magazine*

# Flagpole Co-conspiracy

*White supremacy and racism are perpetuated by White people,
so the only way it's really ever going to end is if we end it.
We can't expect Black people to end racism.*

— James Tyson

James Tyson, the White man who helped Bree Newsome, said he felt called to be "something bigger than myself." This is exactly how he evolved from advocate to co-conspirator and went on to help Newsome over the fence and, upon her descent from the flagpole, stood with her and was arrested alongside her. He committed to something bigger than himself and fulfilled his intention to be a demonstration of what and how White people are called to be and do in support of eradicating racism.

"We never have the conversations we need to have," Tyson said, "which is about racism in America. The reason I felt compelled to get involved with this is because racism in America is perpetuated by White people. Being an informed White person, I feel like I have moral obligation to try to dismantle it."

Racism, inequality, and injustice form our nation's dark shadow. This is ours to eradicate.

We need co-conspirators, people who tap into their divine discomfort and engage their moral obligation to prepare themselves, take a stance, get involved, and do the work required. They knowingly take necessary risks and move outside their comfort and safety zones.

With Tyson, we see and are grateful for his intention and commitment to the greater good. He empowers us to challenge our fears, have the hard conversations, and harness the courage to do what is morally right.

— *Published as the Daily Guide for February 11, 2024,*
Science of Mind *magazine*

# Many Firsts

*I have a great belief in the future of my people and my country.*

— Marian Anderson

I often am in awe of Black folks born at the turn of the 20th century who achieved great success and left a compelling legacy. I marvel at how they persevered and thrived under oppressive racial segregation and animus.

I am awestruck by Marian Anderson, born in 1897. I can only imagine what the full fabric of her life experiences included, among them being the first Black and/or woman to:

- Receive a scholarship from the National Association of Negro Musicians
- Sign with RCA Victor Recording Company and perform solo with the New York Philharmonic
- Perform at the White House in 1936 and solo at the Lincoln Memorial
- Perform on the main stage at the Metropolitan Opera and sing at the inaugurations of Dwight D. Eisenhower and John F. Kennedy
- Be named a Goodwill Ambassador for the U.S. State Department and a delegate to the United Nations

It seems she did it all. She performed at the Lincoln Memorial because the Daughters of the American Revolution denied Howard University's request to hold her concert at Constitution Hall. Eleanor Roosevelt, a DAR member, resigned in protest and formed a committee to find a new venue.

On Easter Sunday, April 9, 1939, on the steps of the Lincoln Memorial, Interior Secretary Harold Ickes introduced Anderson, saying, "Genius draws no color lines." This 25-minute concert is often viewed as a defining moment of the Civil Rights Movement.

Amazingly, by the time of her death in 1993, she had performed at every major concert hall in America.

*—Published as the Daily Guide for February 13, 2024,*
Science of Mind *magazine*

# Sixty Years Ago

*Those who profess to favor freedom, and yet deprecate agitation,
are men who want crops without plowing up the ground.
They want rain without thunder and lightning.*

— Frederick Douglass

In the summer of 2023, we celebrated the sixtieth anniversary of the largest gathering for Civil Rights of its time, the March on Washington for Jobs and Freedom. On August 28, 1963, an estimated 250,000 people assembled at the Washington Monument to protest racial discrimination and promote the pending Civil Rights bill. This was the largest, most diverse, most integrated protest our nation has ever had.

I recently viewed photos from the march. I saw a sea of protest signs and thought, "Sometimes, all we need to see is a sign." The signs read:

*America has a centuries old debt to pay contracted on Emancipation Day.*

*Jobs and Freedom for Every American.*

*End Segregated Rules in Public Schools.*

*Voting Rights Now!*

They foretold a world that works for all, declaring the dreams, visions, and action required for us to live in freedom and justice.

This iconic march was the only one of this magnitude. A sense of oneness prevailed. Hope fueled dreams and fanned the flame of faith. It was a perfect demonstration of our allies, advocates, and co-conspirators walking their talk.

Allies are willing, understanding, accepting, and supportive of our wholeness, freedom, and justice. They demonstrate integrity, empathy, and uprightness. They speak up and stand up. Advocates support and encourage, engaging in "good trouble, necessary trouble." Their advocacy is creative and value-added. They are spokespersons, game changers, and positive influencers.

Co-conspirators always are in the deep end, fully engaged. Their participation assures the objective, often at great personal and professional risk.

At the March on Washington, we were one. Black accord and interracial unity challenged our nation's conscience.

*—Published as the Daily Guide for February 20, 2024,*
Science of Mind *magazine*

## Standing on the Right Side of History

*You have demonstrated over the years that you can stand up in moments of challenge and controversy. One day all of America will be proud of your achievements and will record your work as one of the glowing epics of our heritage.*

— Dr. Martin Luther King Jr., praising Walter Reuther

If you look up some of the Civil Rights leaders shared in these pages, you might wonder who the White guy is in many of the photographs. Without looking, I would respond, "It's probably Walter Reuther," a man fully engaged in the movement. He demonstrated compassionate allyship, focused advocacy, and bold co-conspiracy. He showed up on the right side of history.

Born in 1907, Reuther was a respected organized labor leader and Civil Rights activist. He is credited with leading and expanding the United Auto Workers (UAW) union from 1946 until 1970. He saw labor movements as instruments to advance social justice and human rights in democratic societies, as evidenced in how he leveraged the UAW to advocate for workers' rights, civil rights, women's rights, universal health care, public education, affordable housing, and environmental stewardship.

A powerful ally of Dr. Martin Luther King Jr. and co-conspirator in the Civil Rights Movement, Reuther often marched with King. When protestors were jailed in Birmingham, Reuther arranged $160,000 for their release. He helped organize and finance the 1963 March on Washington, delivering remarks from the steps of the Lincoln Memorial shortly before King gave his historic "I Have a Dream" speech. An early supporter of Cesar Chavez and the United Farm Workers, he got Robert F. Kennedy to visit and support Chavez.

In 1995, U.S. President Bill Clinton posthumously awarded Reuther the Presidential Medal of Freedom, saying, "Walter Reuther was an American visionary so far ahead of his times that although he died a quarter of a century ago, our nation has yet to catch up to his dreams."

*—Published as the Daily Guide for February 23, 2024,*
*Science of Mind magazine*

# More Love, Less Fear

*Blackbird singing in the dead of night,*
*Take these sunken eyes and learn to see*
*All your life, you were only waiting*
*for this moment to be free.*

— Paul McCartney, "Blackbird"

I read that Paul McCartney wrote "Blackbird" about the Civil Rights struggle after reading about American race riots. He said he got "the idea of using a blackbird as a symbol for a Black person. It wasn't necessarily a black 'bird,' but it works that way. ... 'Take these broken wings' was very much in my mind. ... It was purposely symbolic."

McCartney said he penned it in his kitchen in Scotland not long after an incident when the U.S. federal courts forced the racial desegregation of the Little Rock, Arkansas, school system.

It is said that freedom begins in the heart. The Black children sent to Central High in 1957 and their families (the "Little Rock Nine") must have had huge hearts, plus the strength, determination, and courage required to withstand the relentless torment of the racist mobs and other students.

They were on a freedom mission, standing for themselves and others. Watching their plight on the news or in newspaper photos opened many of our eyes and sensitized our hearts. The dignity with which they sought freedom from separate and unequal education offered, " ... liberty to captives, vision to the blind, and to restore the crushed with forgiveness. ..." (Luke 4:18). Empathizing with their vulnerable presence, we were forever changed.

Many of us are still waiting to be free—liberated from ourselves, from our perceived limitations. We yearn for freedom from our patterns of holding ourselves captive and remaining bound to our likes and dislikes, locked in an unwillingness to expand beyond our fears and the past. Freedom from a limiting self-identity is spiritual freedom.

History recorded that the initial attempt to integrate Central High in 1957 did not achieve diversity through integration as intended. In fact, it caused more harm to the people of Little Rock and especially the African-American community than was broadly reported.

It also empowered many of us to challenge commonly accepted limits. This heartbreaking experience continues to inspire us to claim freedom from external forces and to assert and engage it internally. Regardless of circumstances, we are called to freedom—to live from the heart, in more love, less fear.

*—Published in the July 2016* Science of Mind *magazine*

# We Shall Overcome

*What happened in Selma is part of a far larger movement which reaches into every section and State of America. ... It is the effort of American Negroes to secure for themselves the full blessings of American life. Their cause must be our cause, too. Because it is not just Negroes, but really it is all of us who much overcome the crippling legacy of bigotry and injustice. And we shall overcome.*

— U.S. President Lyndon Johnson from his speech, "The American Promise"

Since 1976, every U.S. president has officially designated the month of February as Black History Month. It is our time to acknowledge and honor Black Americans who were and still are summarily omitted from American history books and classes. In truth, Black History contains key elements of our often-unacknowledged shared American history.

I am particularly grateful today for all those who stood, collaborated, and fought for our Civil Rights, often at great personal risk, to improve the plight of Black people by advancing human rights. We have always had allies who consciously and courageously lifted their voices and used their privilege to progress the cause for equal rights. One example is the "We Shall Overcome" speech President Lyndon B. Johnson delivered before a joint session of Congress on March 15, 1965.

He began with these words: "I speak tonight for the dignity of man and the destiny of democracy. I urge every member of both parties, Americans of all religions and of all colors, from every section of this country, to join me in that cause."

At times, history and fate meet in one place to shape a turning point in our unending human search for freedom. So it was at Lexington and Concord. So it was a century ago at Appomattox. So it was in Selma, Alabama. And, I add, so it is today.

President Johnson chose to use his voice and power to gain support for repealing laws that were written to unjustly restrict the freedoms of some Americans. We, too, must engage our prayers, political power, and social influence to change or overturn any laws that perpetuate undermining the human spirit, restricting our basic human rights, and denigrating our innate value. This imbalance is morally wrong and calls us into deeper spiritual practice and pursuit of social justice—not just during Black History Month, but *always*.

—*Published in the February 2017* Science of Mind *magazine*

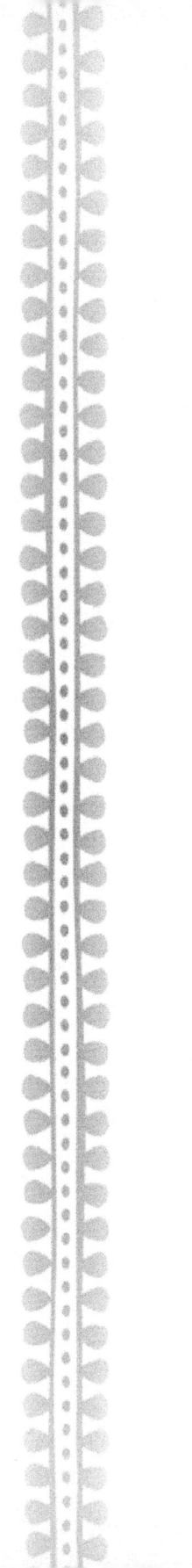

**SECTION 10**

# Good Trouble, Necessary Trouble

## FROM THE INSIDE OUT

*When you see something that is not right, not fair, not just, you have to speak up. You have to say something; you have to do something.*

— John Lewis

# Stand for Our Global Family

The 1989 coverage of protests in Beijing showed a man standing in front of eighteen Chinese tanks and armored carriers in Tiananmen Square (which ironically means "The Gate of Heavenly Peace"). This image became one of the most iconic of all time. Even after thirty years, "Tank Man" remains a mystery and a global symbol of courage and freedom.

The lyrics from "Stand" by Donnie McClurkin may help us demystify:
*Tell me what do you do when you've done all you can*
*And it seems like you can't make it through?*
*Child, you just stand, you just stand, stand*
*Don't you dare give up through the storm*
*Stand through the rain*
*Through the hurt*
*Yeah, through the pain.*

Sometimes, our most courageous stand is to remain seated. During the Civil Rights Movement, many young people—Black and White—put their lives on the line when they sat at lunch counters in southern cities. They were viciously attacked and arrested, and yet sit-ins continued until lunch counters were desegregated.

In December 1955, Rosa Parks remained seated on a Montgomery, Alabama, bus, defying a bus driver's instructions to give up her seat to a White passenger. She later said that she wasn't physically tired. She was tired of giving in. This act sparked the Montgomery Bus Boycott.

Sometimes refusing to stand is required. In 2016, we observed Colin Kaepernick sitting and eventually taking a knee during the national anthem. When asked, he said, "I am not going to stand up to show pride in a flag for a country that oppresses Black people and People of Color. ... To me, this is bigger than football, and it would be selfish on my part to look the other way." Now numerous professional athletes stay in the locker room during the anthem, stand with arms linked, sit it out, or kneel in unified protest.

On this complex adventure in faith called life, I am grateful Centers for Spiritual Living stands boldly committed to a world that works for everyone and for all of creation.

I pray, through the guidance of spiritual wisdom, we each find and take our individual and collective stand to live and grow as one global family, honoring our kinship with all life.

—*Published in the May 2021* Science of Mind *magazine*

## Unbought and Unbossed

These times call for unorthodox ways of transmuting our fears into faith, our doubts into innovation. Allow me to introduce you to a maverick personified: the Honorable Shirley Chisholm. She was a politician, educator, and author who was independent, unbought, and unbossed—fearless. As the first Black woman elected to the U.S. Congress, Representative Chisholm's demonstrated her fearlessness in her political resiliency, determination, and compassionate insight. She exhibited the fortitude to transcend many obstacles and several attempts to quiet her voice.

Born and raised in Brooklyn, she began her nonconformist, history-making ascent as a changemaker. Elected to the New York Assembly in 1965, she lobbied for unemployment insurance for domestic workers and against literacy tests skewed to the disadvantage of those for whom English was not their primary language. Her winning campaign slogan was "Unbought and Unbossed." This maverick platform paved her way to earning a reputation for transforming setbacks into opportunities. As a freshman in Congress, she initially objected to her placement on the House Agricultural Committee as irrelevant, yet through her willingness to collaborate, she used her position to gain access to surplus food to help feed the hungry.

Chisolm had guts. She made a historic run for president in 1972. She said that she did not run to be the first Black president or the first female president. She ran because she wanted to use the platform to advocate for what was needed and what was possible.

Her advocacy for the marginalized and neglected still serves the greater population through our national food stamp (SNAP) program and Nutrition Program for Women, Infants and Children. Both remain indispensable to many Americans living on the economic fringe.

A mindful and fiercely independent thinker, Chisholm transformed political opponents into allies. Her hospital visit with George Wallace, soon after the 1972 attempt on his life, created quite a backlash. Later, after her compassionate outreach, Wallace helped gain the votes of enough Southern congressmen to push Chisholm's legislation through the House. Known for her candor and clarity, Chisholm taught college students to avoid polarization and intolerance, saying, "If you don't accept others who are different, it means nothing that you've learned calculus." And so it is.

*—Published in the June 2020* Science of Mind *magazine*

# Good Samaritan

*A man does what he must—in spite of personal consequences,
in spite of obstacles and dangers and pressures—
and that is the basis of all human morality.*

— U.S. President John F. Kennedy, *Profiles in Courage*

There is something exceptional about people who go way out of their way to assist and support folks in need. It's a current-day Good Samaritan scenario: someone left in desperate need, after certain abuse, rejection, and abandonment, and then the timely appearance and focused attention of someone who responds to divine discomfort with the intention and commitment to make a positive difference. Many debate whether our modern-day Samaritan is taking unnecessary risks or would be better served letting someone else address the situation.

Attorney Bryan Stevenson, founder and Executive Director of the Equal Justice Initiative (EJI), strikes me as a modern-day Good Samaritan. His commitment to justice for those who have been locked up and whose keys have been thrown away is evidenced in his perseverance and dedication to acknowledging everyone's humanity.

"I came from a world where we valued redemption over revenge," he says. Under his leadership, EJI has won major legal challenges eliminating excessive and unfair sentencing, exonerating innocent death-row prisoners, confronting abuse of the incarcerated and the mentally ill, aiding children prosecuted as adults, and protecting condemned prisoners suffering from dementia.

Stevenson and his staff have won reversals, relief, or release from prison for more than 135 wrongly condemned death-row prisoners and relief for hundreds of others wrongly convicted or unfairly sentenced.

"Each person in our society is more than the worst thing they've ever done," he says. He demonstrates principle, is God-sent for so many, and is my spiritual hero.

—*Published as the Daily Guide for February 16, 2024,*
*Science of Mind magazine*

# National Memorial for Peace and Justice

*Sometimes we're fractured by the choices we make; sometimes we're shattered by things we would never have chosen. But our brokenness is also the source of our common humanity, the basis for our shared search for comfort, meaning, and healing. Our shared vulnerability and imperfection nurtures and sustains our capacity for compassion.*

— Bryan Stevenson

The Equal Justice Initiative offices in Montgomery, Alabama, are near where slaves were unloaded at the Alabama River, an area said to be one of the largest slave auction sites in the country. Bryan Stevenson says there were dozens of historic markers and monuments commemorating Confederate history in Montgomery, but nothing acknowledging the history of slavery.

To commemorate those enslaved, Stevenson acquired six acres in Montgomery for the National Memorial for Peace and Justice. The memorial opened in April 2018 and commemorates more than 4,000 who were lynched. He draws a corollary between this traumatic history and how racial bias manifests in disproportionately high mass-incarceration rates.

Associated with the Memorial is the Legacy Museum: From Enslavement to Mass Incarceration. Reconciliation and healing require that we acknowledge and remember the past. "We think it's important that truth and justice work become local," Stevenson says, "and that every community that has witnessed the horror of lynching reckons with that history through memorialization."

In 2022, a new sculpture, "Arise," was installed. I am honored that my likeness is included in artist Branly Cadet's historic sculpture, representing thousands of people nationwide engaged in community remembrance work.

These memorials stand as reminders that the horrors of slavery, the false freedom that followed, and the reprehensible treatment of Black people under the criminal justice system are inextricably related. They also serve as a testament to the resilience, courage, and determination of Black people to persevere, no matter what.

*—Published as the Daily Guide for February 17, 2024,*
Science of Mind *magazine*

# Rest in Power

*A democracy cannot thrive where power remains unchecked and justice is reserved for a select few. Ignoring these cries and failing to respond to this movement is simply not an option—for peace cannot exist where justice is not served.*

— John Lewis

Long before he became a renowned American politician and Civil Rights activist, serving in the U.S. Congress from 1987 until his death in 2020, John Lewis participated in the 1960 Nashville sit-ins and the Freedom Rides. He was chairman of the Student Nonviolent Coordinating Committee from 1963 to 1966.

He also was one of the "Big Six" organizers of the 1963 March on Washington. In 1965, John Lewis led the first Selma to Montgomery march across Edmund Pettus Bridge. On "Bloody Sunday" in 1965, state troopers attacked marchers on the bridge, and Lewis was gravely injured. Even that did not stop him; his commitment endured.

In 1963, Rep. John Lewis was known as "the boy from Troy." He was just twenty-three years old when he delivered a rousing speech and call to action during the March on Washington. Even then, he knew and told us:

*To those who have said, "Be patient and wait," we have long said that we cannot be patient. We do not want our freedom gradually, but we want to be free now! We are tired. We are tired of being beaten by policemen. We are tired of seeing our people locked up in jail over and over again. ...*

*We do not want to go to jail. But we will go to jail if this is the price we must pay for love, brotherhood, and true peace. ... Wake up America! Wake up, for we cannot stop, and we will not and cannot be patient.*

Lewis's committed activism continues to challenge each of us to get into what he called "good trouble, necessary trouble."

—Published as the Daily Guide for February 24, 2024, Science of Mind *magazine*

# A Dream and a Call to Stay Woke

*Make a career of humanity. Commit yourself to the noble struggle
for equal rights. You will make a better person of yourself,
a greater nation of your country, and a finer world to live in.*

— Dr. Martin Luther King Jr.

Martin Luther King Jr.'s enduring legacy encompasses leadership, inspiration, and mobilization of the broadest possible constituency against racism and social injustice.

In 1968, just as legislation he fought for was finally coming to fruition, he was assassinated. I am always stunned to recall he was only thirty-nine years old. He spent his brief adulthood preaching faith, fairness, dignity, brotherhood, and justice. Eighteen years after his assassination, his birthday became a national holiday.

King is remembered and acclaimed for his March on Washington and his "I Have a Dream" speech, and for his final sermon, in which he declared that he might not "get to the mountaintop." He gave an early version of his "Dream" speech at the Walk to Freedom, a mass march in Detroit, Michigan, on June 23, 1963, where demonstrators protested racism, discrimination, segregation, and the brutalization of Civil Rights activists. It was also a dress rehearsal for the March on Washington, scheduled for two months later.

On March 31, 1968, King unknowingly preached his last sermon, "Remaining Awake Through a Great Revolution." He reminded listeners that Rip Van Winkle slept through the American Revolution. He prophetically spoke of a "triple revolution: … a technological revolution with the impact of automation and cybernation; … a revolution in weaponry with the emergence of atomic and nuclear weapons of warfare; … the human rights revolution with the freedom explosion that is taking place all over the world."

He implored us not to sleep through these revolutions, saying, "Many fail to develop the new attitudes, the new mental responses that the new situation demands. They end up sleeping through a revolution."

His advice to "stay woke" serves us well.

*—Published as the Daily Guide for February 12, 2024,* Science of Mind *magazine*

## SECTION II

# Our Stories

## FROM THE INSIDE OUT

*The Mis-Education of the Negro, in which Carter G. Woodson explains that in the American education system, the entirety of Black people's existence "is studied only as a problem or dismissed as of little consequence."*

— Michael Harriot

# Black History Is American History

*The only difference between a burglar and a "settler" is who writes the police reports.*

— Michael Harriot

It helps to know and hold in context what it was that Black historical figures were getting over. It helps to have a clear context of the time, laws, culture, and power dynamics to better understand what was required for Black folks to succeed.

My research reveals an upward striving based in determination, perseverance, tremendous faith, courage beyond what I have seen or known, unconditional love, open heartedness, compassion, and empathy. This striving seems the catalyst that drove these historical figures from what might have been their destiny, had they bought into the constraints forced on them.

Instead, they nurtured and harvested a larger vision, a healthy sense of self, a divine knowing that something more was possible and ultimately inevitable. And they didn't stop there. They stayed the course and worked to create a way out of no way.

This can be instructional for all of us, to acknowledge and honor their horrendous circumstances and immense risks. Although many did not make it to the mountaintop, they never gave up. And many thrived.

I am blessed to see myself and this teaching—the principles we teach and endeavor to practice—evidenced throughout these stories.

All sustainable progress depends on us working together toward our collective greater good. Some will be resistant. Some will serve and support as allies, some as advocates. And some will step up as co-conspirators, committed to doing whatever it takes, including what the Honorable John Lewis called getting into "good trouble, necessary trouble."

—Published as the Daily Guide for February 1, 2024, Science of Mind *magazine*

## And So It Began...

*The life of a nation is secure only while the nation is honest, truthful, and virtuous.*

— Frederick Douglass

My ancestors survived the Middle Passage. Some crossed the Atlantic Ocean chained to other humans, many sick or dying for months, in the hulls of disease-infested ships. Stripped of their cultural and personal dignity, they were sold immediately upon landing.

This peculiar institution—chattel slavery—was brutally torturous. Women and men were raped, maimed, beaten, and killed. Newborns were snatched from their mothers' arms and sold, while the mothers became wet nurses for White newborns. Renamed, they surrendered their heritage, picked up essential words from the local vernacular, and some risked their lives to learn to read and write.

I am grateful to be. I know only the strong in mind, body, and spirit survived. I come from these people. We are among those who refused to die. Once emancipated, those who survived the horrors of slavery were again enslaved by an intentional poverty cycle of sharecropping, a penal system designed to provide free labor, the calculated terror of the Ku Klux Klan, and the recurrent anguish of mutilated Black bodies hanging from trees.

After the Civil War, we fought in wars, boycotted, sat-in, rode buses, and marched in hope of securing equal rights. We were met with violent threats, firehoses, vicious dogs, burning crosses, beatings, incarcerations, and assassinations. These racist actions continue to morph, now being tweaked for the 21st century.

I am and we are our ancestors—the ones enslaved, those who enslaved, the ones who escaped, the ones who assisted, and those who hindered. We are the ones who survived, the ones who have a human right to thrive. I tell our stories because each of them is about all of us.

—*Published as the Daily Guide for February 2, 2024,*
Science of Mind *magazine*

# Trek Into Darkness

*The injustices endured by Black Americans at the hands of
their own government have no parallel in our history, not only
during the period of slavery but also in the Jim Crow era that followed.*

— Jim Webb

For me, Black history is a source of ever-increasing pride, awareness, clarity, access, and focus. We could break Google if we were to include the complete story of the African role in establishing the British Colonies and the wealth-economy of these United States. It also would require a trek into darkness.

Our true history is rife with invalidating and discrediting the wisdom, intellect, and ingenuity of the enslaved. Black history, at its best, illuminates a legacy of faith, love, and perseverance. It returns us to wholeness. It also exposes an intentional culture of inequity and exclusion, terror and brutality.

My research and writing about Black history immersed me in feelings I suspect are linked to generational trauma. This project, to write the Daily Guides for the February 2024 issue of *Science of Mind* magazine, triggered the trauma of being Black in America, while increasing my awareness of our racial history. The task proved challenging and exhilarating, inspiring and triggering. These writings are my North Star to freedom and historical truths.

I am aware of how difficult it is to comprehend stories of triumph without a sense of the circumstances from which these triumphs reigned. So I am excited to share some "how I got over" stories. What our protagonists "got over" often was the most uncomfortable part—the divine discomfort—within their stories. We must engage our intuitive discernment to see within and beyond the suffering, to glean the deep faith, courage, discipline, determination, wisdom, and love.

I fully understand this may be read through a completely different lens by those less aware of America's authentic history and ethnicity-based laws and policies. I especially request grace and open heartedness from those for whom that is the case.

— *Published as the Daily Guide for February 3, 2024,*
Science of Mind *magazine*

# A New Origin Story

*We hold these truths to be self-evident, that all men are created equal, that they are endowed by their Creator with certain unalienable Rights, that among these are Life, Liberty, and the pursuit of Happiness.*

— Thomas Jefferson, *Declaration of Independence*

It was a game changer for me: *The 1619 Project: A New Origin Story.* The subtitle of the book, "a new origin story," is exactly how I received and filed it. This new origin story of the United States shifted my awareness and sense of my place and my people's role in history. The origin of America and the people of African ancestry's contribution are inextricably intertwined.

The first record of enslaved Africans in America was when the White Lion dropped anchor in the British colony of Jamestown, Virginia, in 1619. This was a year before the Mayflower landed in 1620.

This previously concealed history, now publicly exposed, reveals the impossibility of separating chattel slavery from our American economy, an economy built on the backs of the enslaved and documented as early as 1619. There is no legacy of the American wealth economy without slavery. The truth is that our current American economy is based on wealth generated during slavery.

It was built on a foundation of enslaving Africans to create a "new prosperous world."

Too many learn late in life the degree to which African people contributed—as enslaved people—to the "greatest economy in the world." Key to how we understand who we are and our place in the world are our stories—stories of and about where we came from, what we have contributed, the past on which we now stand, and the awareness from which we launch our future.

I see why this history was hidden in plain sight and not universally taught.

— *Published as the Daily Guide for February 4, 2024,*
Science of Mind *magazine*

# 1619: Oneness Is Not Sameness

*A battle lost or won is easily described, understood, and appreciated, but the moral growth of a great nation requires reflection, as well as observation, to appreciate it.*

— Frederick Douglass

I'm reminded by *The 1619 Project* that oneness is not sameness and that we each have our individual and ancestral points of origin. Our point of origin in any experience is unique, encompassing the significance of how we got here and how our lives got to be the way they are. This is true for us individually, as well as for America.

In addition to our cultural-historical mindsets and practices, we each bring different belief systems, values, and cultural norms. Because it is done unto us as we believe, being led to believe that those of African ancestry have less or no value and should be treated as such, negatively impacts our sense of who we are—our sense of our worthiness, capabilities, and ability to contribute to the greater good.

Until we set straight, acknowledge, and respect everyone's origin story, we remain at the effect of the oppressor's power and gaze.

The notion of changing your thinking to change your life also applies to our nation's consciousness in terms of how we see the oppressor and the oppressed, how we hold African Americans, and how we see and hold and often reinforce the origin stories of White Americans.

In our pursuit of truth and discerning ancestral and historical cause, we must seek and embrace an accurate world history. When appropriately honored and accurately represented, this history allows us to focus on, pursue, and uncover our true shared past.

Only then can we hope to understand. Once understood, our shared past and original points of connection are certain to reveal how our current reality is the logical outcome of our beliefs, practices, and treatment of each other.

—Published as the Daily Guide for February 5, 2024,
Science of Mind *magazine*

# A Sinister Bet

*Every man knows that slavery is a curse.*
*Whoever denies this, his lips libel his heart.*

— Theodore Dwight Weld

Truth often is stranger than fiction. In 1859, Timothy Meaher, a White wealthy human trafficker, made a bet. He wagered "a thousand dollars that inside two years I myself can bring a ship full of ni**ers right into Mobile Bay under the officers' noses."

He sent his slave ship, the Clotilda, to buy and transport captives from Dahomey (present day Benin). The crew returned to Mobile Bay with 110 African men, women, and children, and under cover of darkness, smuggled them into Mobile, Alabama. Meaher illegally sold some of the enslaved and took the rest for his brother and himself. He directed the ship's captain, William Foster, to burn and scuttle the ship to conceal this sinister crime.

Meaher committed this crime fifty years after the "Act Prohibiting the Importation of Slaves" took effect in 1808, making it illegal for Americans to engage in the international slave trade. Violators who transported slaves risked arrest, fines, seizure of their ships, and confiscation of their cargo.

The U.S. government attempted to charge Meaher, but he was never held accountable. Two years before his death in 1890, Meaher bragged in a newspaper interview about having masterminded this crime.

The Clotilda was the last known slave ship to bring African captives to the United States. The buried wreckage of this ship was located and retrieved in 2019. Some may wonder, as I do, why it took 159 years to definitively establish this crime and confirm the identity of the perpetrators.

—*Published as the Daily Guide for February 26, 2024,*
Science of Mind *magazine*

# Jim Crow Code

*The history of African American repression in this country rose from government-sanctioned racism. Jim Crow laws were a product of bigoted state and local governments.*

— U.S. Senator Rand Paul

While researching the story about the slave ship Clotilda and how the government could not prove Meaher's crime, I discerned an established and historical pattern of racist obfuscation. This troubling pattern, in which Whites can terrorize Blacks with lynching, rape, arson but without legal consequences, supported an entire culture of oppression.

I refer to this pattern as the "Jim Crow Code." It is fundamentally deep-seated and dangerous:

1. Do dastardly deeds under a cloak of invisibility and anonymity. Think: Klu Klux Klan.

2. Invoke the generational code of silence and secrecy. This is essential. Having done the deed, successfully deny it, and then skirt the legal consequence. Think: Emmett Till's murder.

3. Gaslight anyone who pierces the veil and dares speaks truth to oppression. Instead, ask, "Why are you still talking about the past?" Think: Any slavery reference or assassination.

This consistent pattern of oppression, validating the Jim Crow Code, allows the truth to hide in plain sight. It was common knowledge that the Clotilda brought the African captives to Mobile, that the ship was then sunk by Captain Foster, that Timothy Meaher initiated this voyage and acquisition, intentionally breaking the law, and that the general location of the sunken ship was just off Meaher's land. The crew was silenced, disbanded, and dispatched North to minimize exposure, the criminals never held to account.

We need allies, advocates, and co-conspirators willing to break rank, expose the deeds, and dismantle the false narratives. We must disrupt these destructive multigenerational patterns.

*—Published as the Daily Guide for February 27, 2024,*
*Science of Mind magazine*

# Oluale Kossola and Africatown

*All these words from the seller, but not one word from the sold...*
*the thoughts of the "black ivory," the "coin of Africa," had no market value.*
*Africa's ambassadors to the New World have come and worked and died,*
*and left their spoor, but no recorded thought.*

— Zora Neale Hurston, *Barracoon: The Story of the Last "Black Cargo"*

The radical power of history is on display in the Netflix documentary, "Descendant," about Africatown and the Clotilda slave ship, and in Florida's and other states' ongoing campaigns to erase history.

Africatown is a historic community located just north of Mobile, Alabama. It was formed by a group of thirty-two West Africans, who in 1860 were trafficked in the last known illegal shipment of Africans, enslaved until the end of the Civil War, and freed in 1865 by the Emancipation Proclamation. They bought land, founded, and created their own community—Africatown, Alabama.

I first learned of Africatown and its leader, Cudjo Lewis née Oluale Kossola, through Zora Neale Hurston's published interview with him. Lewis lived until 1935 and was thought to be the last survivor of the Clotilda living in Africatown. In the interview, Lewis recalls his violent abduction from Togo, his voyage aboard the Clotilda, and his enslavement by Timothy Meaher. He revealed much about the Togo culture from which the Dahomey warriors seized him. He yearned for his homeland.

Africatown founders retained their West African customs and language, while their children and some elders also learned English. Africatown is the only American community created by West Africans who survived the Middle Passage.

From 1860 to 2019, when the Clotilda wreckage was retrieved, equals 169 years of deception and denial. Attempts to hide the story failed, as descendants in Africatown and the Mobile area continue to preserve their families' legacies. Finally, in 2022, the Meaher family called the actions of Timothy Meaher "evil and unforgivable," recognizing his actions had "consequences that have impacted generations of people."

—*Published as the Daily Guide for February 25, 2024,*
*Science of Mind* magazine

# Spiritual and Genetic Siblings

*The Unity of Good is a revelation of the greatest importance, for it teaches us that we are one with the whole, and one with each other. This realization alone will settle the question of human inequality.*

— Ernest Holmes

As Centers for Spiritual Living, we are blessed to know, accept, and embrace our oneness in God and ever expand our willingness to discern, acknowledge, and affirm the divinity of our fellow humans and ourselves. However, this principle of oneness may not be as readily accessible and undeniably real for everyone.

This was evident during my visit to the National Museum of African-American History and Culture in Washington, D.C. This Smithsonian Museum chronicles African-American history from the arrival of the first Africans, well preceding the "peculiar institution" of slavery, through the advent of the Black Lives Matter movement. I experienced two intense days taking in "A people's journey, a nation's history." It confirmed and illuminated how essential and deeply ingrained my ancestors are in the core fabric of this country, and I am forever changed in my sense of the breadth and scope of my generational bond to America and all its inhabitants.

As an American of obvious African ancestry, I am aware and have historical and genetic confirmation that I also have European ancestors. This is not unique to me, as the average African-American genome is said to be nearly a quarter European, and almost 4 percent of European-Americans are reported to have African ancestry.

So spiritually and genetically, we are brothers and sisters—bonafide kin. Worshiping at the altar of separateness and the social construct of race is foolhardy and perilous behavior. *We are one.*

If only the following words from Holmes reflected our current experience: "This realization [of oneness] alone will settle the question of human inequality. The real Fatherhood of God and the Actual brotherhood of Man will be made apparent on Earth to the degree that men realize True Unity." [capitalization original]

This is key to our freedom and is our revelation of true unity.

—Published in the February 2018 *Science of Mind* magazine

# *We Must Face Our Fear*

*Because ours is a firmly entrenched system in which the roots of white supremacy run deep ... it is critical that we all grab a shovel. To do anything less would be absolutely unforgivable.*

— John Oliver

I love John Oliver's use of the shovel as a metaphor. No one grabs a shovel without the intent to put it to good use. This is a clarion call to face our fear and put our intentions and principles to good use. As we welcome autumn, we recall how this past spring, the United States was ravaged by the Covid-19 pandemic and the endemic of racism. Two deadly viruses—one new and one that has festered as a national wound for centuries. This double crisis formed a perfect storm for introspection, prayer, and action. The scab of denial and spiritual bypass ("thoughts and prayers" and "all lives matter") was removed to expose systemic, racially motivated crimes, and killings, and voter-suppression tactics.

Those committed to learning a more accurate U.S. history, including the authentic legacy of Black folk in America, will come to understand how life got to be the way it is, pick up a shovel, and work toward healing. The nationwide and international marches in protest of the inhumane treatment of Black lives and against police brutality generated increased awareness, empathy, and engagement.

The change we seek is not only seeking us, it is manifesting. Merriam-Webster recently revised its definition of racism after a young Black woman requested it be updated to include the systemic oppression of certain groups of people.

Other changes have been swift and poignant. Transformative conversations affirm that once people know better, they often do better. Some are slower to realize our oneness.

Complaining about Black Lives Matter, someone said, "We are in trouble if we don't realize that all lives matter." That, of course, is the point. We are "in trouble" because we have demonstrated Black lives do not matter through the historic and consistent treatment of our Black brethren. Confronting ignorance requires transcending our fears. As long as Black lives do not matter, all lives do not matter.

Acknowledging this truth, grabbing a shovel, and facing our fears is the path to creating a world that works for all. The truth is Black lives matter. Agree or disagree; just do not change the subject.

*—Published in the September 2020* Science of Mind *magazine*

# *I'm Curious. Are You?*

*We are in the Mind Inexhaustible. The Infinite never rests on Its laurels. It never stops creating for a moment. It expects us to do the same. It expects us to be fully alive, using our curiosity to feed new ideas into our consciousness.*

— Raymond Charles Barker

It's Black History Month, and I wholeheartedly invoke curiosity—a healthy, natural inquisitiveness—as our superpower. It is our nature to wonder, be interested in, be inquisitive about exactly how life evolved as it has. This is the perfect time to grab our capes, seek truth, and reveal a greater possibility. This is our opportunity to use our superpower to expand our awareness of who and whose we are.

Until we foster an authentic and deep curiosity of the Life of God expressing as humanity, we must have at least a minimum amount of inquisitiveness. We must first express a strong, authentic desire to know and learn about each other. "Using our curiosity to feed new ideas into our consciousness," as Raymond Charles Barker states in the above quote, we activate our spirit of inquiry and imagination. This, in turn, activates the principle of inclusivity and a consciousness of oneness with all life, forming the basis of a world that works for all.

It is time for us, as a spiritual community, to lean into our authentic interest in who we are. Even if we do not discern how or when our current way of being with each other was first established and under what circumstances, we are still called to make reparations.

I am curious about the following questions. Are you?

How can we embrace oneness if we do not honor our differences?

- To what degree does it behoove us to inquire about the mental equivalent of enslavement, Jim Crow, racial and gender-based supremacy, and the long-term impact of each?
- What might be the effect of this systemic generational trauma, and what does it mean for us now?
- When will we be sufficiently curious and invested in each other to call forth a world that works for all?

Curiosity and the truth it can reveal is our superpower. It can assist us in discerning our roles and responsibilities—what is ours to be and do. I know this superpower, when fully engaged, yields increased awareness, and awareness changes everything.

*—Published in the February 2023* Science of Mind *magazine*

## SECTION 12

# Our Way Out of No Way

## FROM THE INSIDE OUT

*Freedom is the emancipation from the arbitrary rule of other men.*

— Mortimer J. Adler

# To the Degree We Become Conscious

*Slavery can only be abolished by raising the character of the people who compose the nation; and that can be done only by showing them a higher one.*

— Maria Weston Chapman

CSL's Declaration of Principles says, "We believe that the Kingdom of Heaven is within us and that we experience this Kingdom to the degree that we become conscious of it." Harriet Tubman's life—her beliefs and her fearlessness—offers an example of how we might demonstrate this exalted consciousness in our living. Her life and living reveal the power at the center of her knowing.

Mother Harriet's story is well known. There are books and movies detailing her head injury at an overseer's hands, her determination to be free, and her willingness to risk her life in support of others' freedom. There is something about her that is never fully acknowledged—her determined spirit and resolute faith, her drive to escape and intuitive ability to avoid capture and death at the hands of slave catchers.

The a capella group, Sweet Honey in the Rock, has a song called "I Remember and I Believe." The lyrics say:

> *I don't know how my mother walked her trouble down.*
> *I don't know how my father stood his ground.*
> *I don't know how my people survived slavery.*
> *I do remember, that's why I believe.*

Well, I cannot fathom how Harriet Tubman survived as an enslaved person for more than twenty-five years, ultimately escaping, only to return time and again to free other enslaved persons and to serve as a trusted spy for the Union Army.

She is my hero, a champion of those othered and dehumanized. I lift her up as the epitome of inner knowing, clear intention, endurance, and freedom. Her sense of personal responsibility and justice freed so many, then and now.

—Published as the Daily Guide for February 6, 2024,
Science of Mind *magazine*

# Seven Years

*Whenever I hear anyone arguing for slavery,*
*I feel a strong impulse to see it tried on him personally.*

— U.S. President Abraham Lincoln

I have heard that the number seven is related to our spiritual journey and may foretell a spiritual awakening. I do not know whether this is so. I do know, however, that Harriet Jacobs's seven years in hiding led to an amazing shift in her life and circumstances.

Born enslaved in 1813, she suffered the trauma of being abused, sold, and moved between owners, giving birth, having her children enslaved, and witnessing some being sold. She had the utmost faith in God and believed God would be her rescuer. She relied on and exemplified an abiding faith that her condition and circumstance could and would change. Eventually, she escaped.

What is most unique about Jacobs is that once free, she wrote *Incidents in the Life of a Slave Girl*, documenting her experience as a slave in North Carolina. She is the only woman known to have left papers testifying to her life while enslaved. Her autobiography stands as an essential slave narrative.

Jacobs suffered in her enslaved circumstance until she made the decision to be free. In June 1835, she escaped. For a short time, she found safe harbor with various Black and White neighbors. When she realized she could not make it to freedom, she returned and hid in a crawl space above her grandmother's porch. She stayed there—self-imprisoned under a tin roof, freezing cold in the winter and sweltering in the summer—for seven years.

Then came a shift—an opening—through which she successfully escaped. Once in Rochester, New York, she became an active abolitionist.

I am enriched and inspired by Jacobs' perseverance and willingness to tell her story.

—Published as the Daily Guide for February 7, 2024,
Science of Mind *magazine*

## *Awareness Can Be Curative*

*Who talks most about freedom and equality? Is it not those who hold a Bill of Rights in one hand and a whip for affrighted slaves in the other?*

— Alexander Hamilton

From 1790 until 1797, President George Washington resided in the temporary seat of the nation's capital, Philadelphia. Pennsylvania law required enslaved people be set free after six months of residency in the state. Rather than comply, Washington circumvented the law. Every six months he sent his slaves down South, just as the clock was about to expire.

Ona Judge was one of his slaves. Born at Mount Vernon around 1774, when the opportunity presented itself, she escaped during dinner service on May 21, 1796. Many were incredulous that she could and would leave the Washingtons' enslavement. Judge became the subject of an intense manhunt run by President Washington, who used his political and personal contacts to recapture her.

Although enculturated to obey Whites, Judge stood her ground when pressured to return to slavery. She said she looked Washington's agent straight in the eyes—her response final and courageous—and said, "I am free now and choose to remain so." Washington was a powerful man, yet she stood up to his agent on her newfound ground, rejecting his demands and the legal system of slavery.

Harriet Tubman said, "I could have freed more people, if only they had known they were enslaved." Well, Judge knew she had been enslaved, and she knew she wanted more. She demonstrated faith, wisdom, and determination. She clearly read the writing on the wall, realizing if she stayed, she could be forever enslaved. She chose freedom.

Ona Judge Staines died on February 25, 1848, in Greenland, New Hampshire, a free woman.

*—Published as the Daily Guide for February 14, 2024,*
Science of Mind *magazine*

# Now Is the Time to Be Free

*Oh freedom, oh freedom,*
*Oh freedom over me*
*And before I'd be a slave*
*I'll be buried in my grave*
*And go home to my Lord and be free.*

— African-American song, "Oh Freedom"

In the Oscar-winning film based on a true story, *Twelve Years a Slave,* one of the characters says to Solomon Northup, "If you want to survive, say as little as possible." Solomon's immediate reply is, "I do not want to survive; I want to live!" Over the twelve years he was enslaved, he never let go of his intention to live free.

I cannot imagine what Solomon, along with many inmates incarcerated for crimes they did not commit, must tell themselves to maintain their sanity and clarity of intent. I do know, however, that our inner dialogue and belief patterns lay the tracks of our lives, and once we lay the track, our life runs along it toward the manifest equivalent of our thoughts, feelings, attitudes, and beliefs.

This takes Ernest Holmes's definition of freedom to another level: "Freedom means to eliminate from consciousness all those things that bind and limit the free flowing of the Divine Spirit through us and, at the same time, to exercise the faculty of personal choice." Anyone physically imprisoned or enslaved, or bound by an indeterminate sentence of guilt and shame, must realize their innate value and create a deep inner sense and engagement of their "faculty of personal choice" toward their highest good.

Regardless of how we were bound, we must begin to consistently perceive ourselves as free. Emmet Fox seems to up the ante when he admonishes us to "change your thinking and leave it changed." For the one who experiences freedom, as the song lyrics above suggest, being permeated with such a high consciousness of freedom that you are already free in mind and spirit, that person has already ceased identifying as bound and instead perceives, with ever-increasing faith and commitment, the freedom that she already is. Once you raise your consciousness, you elevate your life. Choose to be free.

—Published in the July 2014 *Science of Mind* magazine

# *I Am Every Woman*

*May I say a few words? I want to say a few words about this matter. I am a woman's rights. I have as much muscle as any man, and can do as much work as any man. I have plowed and reaped and husked and chopped and mowed, and can any man do more than that?*

— Sojourner Truth, May 29, 1851

In 1797, Isabella Bomfree was born into slavery in Swartekill, Ulster County, New York, and, with her infant daughter, escaped in 1826 to freedom. She was a charismatic speaker who lifted her voice as a committed abolitionist and women's rights activist. In 1843, she proclaimed that Spirit called her to preach the truth and renamed herself Sojourner Truth.

In 1851, Truth began a lecture tour that included a women's rights conference in Akron, Ohio. Standing at nearly six feet tall, she delivered a speech in which she challenged prevailing notions of racial and gender inferiority and inequality. Truth advocated for immediate change in voting status and ultimately split with those, including Frederick Douglass, who believed suffrage for formerly enslaved men should precede women's suffrage.

While the prevailing culture of that time saw her as less than and treated her as unworthy, she continuously fought this and stood up for herself as a person, a woman, a woman of color, and a citizen. And she fought for all others as fully human and worthy of justice and liberty.

Not enough has changed since 1851. Truth's story is our collective story even now. Her struggle to define herself as wholly human and worthy of freedom is still present for us. We cannot allow Sojourner Truth to become a myth or a one-dimensional character. It is crucial that we embrace her as a fully orbed person—a divine being who, despite beginning life enslaved, escaped and worked tirelessly with unconditional love and remarkable courage toward human rights for all.

Truth's audacious declaration, "I am a woman's rights," is a call for all of us to stand for human rights. From an intention to fully embrace the divine feminine in all and through self-realization, regardless of gender identification, all of us can come to realize, we ARE every woman.

—Published in the March 2020 *Science of Mind* magazine

# *In Pursuit of Freedom*

*Now let us begin. Now let us rededicate ourselves to the long and bitter—but beautiful—struggle for a new world.*

— Rev. Dr. Martin Luther King Jr.

We arrived to this country from every corner of the Earth. We came seeking freedom like moths seek a candle's flame, on an adventure in faith and in pursuit of a new world.

The North Star (Polaris) served many courageous souls escaping the scourge of slavery in the United States in their pursuit of freedom. There were whispers and songs advising escapees to "Follow the Drinking Gourd" (the Big Dipper). Always, Divine Spirit and Principle urged them forward, lit their paths, illuminated possibilities and access to a new life.

The slave narratives and even recent immigrant testimonies reveal that our migration and immigration in pursuit of freedom require a consciousness of courage, faith, perseverance, fortitude, ingenuity, and flexibility. This is how legions of humans—legally enslaved, yet determined to be free—escaped the inhumanity of slavery.

A century later, in order to dislodge the humiliating and debilitating Jim Crow boot from their necks, Black folk engaged principle, stood courageously, and joined the exodus out of the South. Across time and space, they rejected their dire circumstances in pursuit of the equality, liberty, freedom, and happiness promised in the preamble of Science of Mind's Declaration of Principles.

The stakes in this pursuit of freedom are high, often a life-or-death equation. Even so, we do not give up. Circa 1859, Harriet Tubman declared with deep conviction, "There are two things I've got a right to, and these are death or liberty. One or the other I mean to have. No one will take me back alive. I shall fight for my liberty, and when the time has come for me to go, the Lord will let them kill me."

Faith and the courage to act are essential to claim freedom, and Harriet Tubman is an exemplar of personal power, deep consistent faith, and extraordinary, courageous action. Indeed, as the Rev. Halford Luccock reminds us, "Where there is no faith in the future, there is no power in the present."

—*Published in the February 2021* Science of Mind *magazine*

# APPENDIX A:
# CENTERS FOR SPIRITUAL LIVING VISION STATEMENT

We envision all people, all beings, and all life as expressions of God.

We see a world in which each and every person lives in alignment with their highest spiritual principle, emphasizing unity with God and connection with each other; a world in which individually and collectively we are called to a higher state of consciousness and action.

We envision humanity awakening to its spiritual magnificence and discovering the creative power of thought; a world where each and every person discovers their own personal power and ability to create an individual life that works within a world that works for everyone.

We envision a world in which we live and grow as One Global Family that respects and honors the interconnectedness of all life; a world where this kinship with all life prospers and connects through the guidance of spiritual wisdom and experience.

We envision a world where personal responsibility joins with social conscience in every area of the political, corporate, academic, and social sectors, providing sustainable structures to further the emerging global consciousness.

We envision a world where each and every person has enough food, a home and a sense of belonging; a world of peace and harmony, enfranchisement and justice.

We envision a world in which resources are valued, cared for, and grown, and where there is generous and continuous sharing of these resources.

We envision a worldwide culture in which forgiveness (whether for errors, injustices, or debts) is the norm.

We envision a world which has renewed its emphasis on beauty, nature, and love through the resurgence of creativity, art, and aesthetics.

We envision a world that works for everyone and for all of creation.

# APPENDIX B:
## CSL DECLARATION OF PRINCIPLES

WE BELIEVE in God, the Living Spirit Almighty; one, indestructible, absolute, and self-existent Cause. This One manifests Itself in and through all creation, but is not absorbed by Its creation. The manifest universe is the body of God; it is the logical and necessary outcome of the infinite self-knowingness of God.

WE BELIEVE in the individualization of the Spirit in us, and that all people are individualizations of the One Spirit.

WE BELIEVE in the eternality, the immortality, and the continuity of the individual soul, forever and ever expanding.

WE BELIEVE that heaven is within us, and that we experience it to the degree that we become conscious of it.

WE BELIEVE the ultimate goal of life to be a complete emancipation from all discord of every nature, and that this goal is sure to be attained by all.

WE BELIEVE in the unity of all life, and that the highest God and the innermost God is one God. We believe that God is personal to all who feel this indwelling presence.

WE BELIEVE in the direct revelation of truth through our intuitive and spiritual nature, and that anyone may become a revealer of truth who lives in close contact with the indwelling God.

WE BELIEVE that the Universal Spirit, which is God, operates through a Universal Mind, which is the Law of God; and that we are surrounded by this Creative Mind, which receives the direct impress of our thought and acts upon it.

WE BELIEVE in the healing of the sick and control of conditions through the power of this Mind.

WE BELIEVE in the eternal Goodness, the eternal Loving-kindness, and the eternal Givingness of Life to All.

WE BELIEVE in our own soul, our own spirit, and our own destiny; for we understand that the life of all is God.

*—Written by Ernest Holmes and published in the first issue of*
Science of Mind *magazine, October 1927*

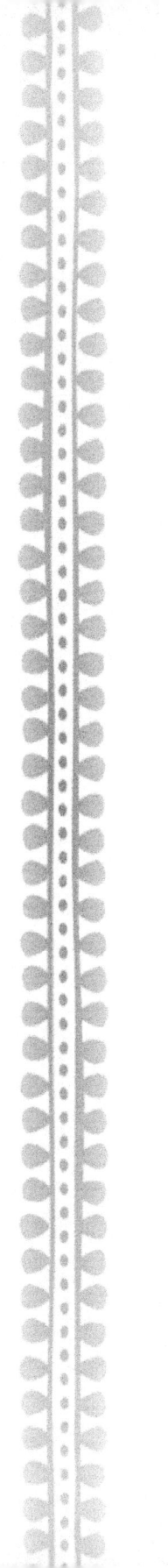

# About the Author

Rev. Dr. Andriette Earl is an inspiring and respected leader, life coach, author, composer, and teacher with decades of experience in both corporate and spiritual settings. Locally and globally, she has engaged thousands in conscious and intentional living through the adoption of proven spiritual practices.

In 2009, she founded Heart and Soul Center of Light (HSCL), a Centers for Spiritual Living (CSL) affiliate and vibrant, world-class teaching and empowerment ministry.

As a teacher, Rev. Dr. Andriette embraces creative spiritual processes to support self-actualization and transformation. At the Holmes Institute School of Spiritual Leadership, where she has taught for more than a decade, students know her to be mentally energetic and creative, thoughtful in her translation of spiritual principles and practices. The board game she created, "Speak Your Word: The Freedom Game," is one of many examples of how she creates ingenious methods to encourage others to expand their consciousness and transform their lives.

Readers of her *Science of Mind* magazine monthly column, From the Inside Out, say she offers "...a tremendous heart, a healing presence, and great enthusiasm for transforming one's life." She is the author of *Embracing Wholeness: Living in Spiritual Congruence* and the creator/producer of HSCL's video blog and podcast, "Point of Power." She also composed lyrics to songs that center our hearts and embrace the powerful intention of our lives.

As a CSL leader, Rev. Dr. Andriette is a sought-after convener, leader, and team builder. She served two terms on the CSL Minister's Council (2016-2023) and as a member of the CSL Leadership Council. She previously served as a visioning facilitator, on CSL's Nominations Committee, the CSL Convention Committee, and the Spiritually Motivated/Socially Engaged team.

Rev. Dr. Andriette holds a master's degree in Consciousness Studies and received an honorary doctorate of divinity in 2021 from Centers for Spiritual Living.

Made in United States
North Haven, CT
28 September 2024